Understanding God Together

•

13 Bible Studies for Youth Ministry

Group
Loveland, Colorado

Understanding God Together:
13 Bible Studies for Youth Ministry

Copyright © 1999 Group Publishing, Inc.

All rights reserved. No part of this book may be reproduced in any manner whatsoever without prior written permission from the publisher, except where noted in the text or in the case of brief quotations embodied in critical articles and reviews. For information, write Permissions, Group Publishing, Inc., Dept. PD, P.O. Box 481, Loveland, CO 80539.

Credits
Authors: Tim Baker, Matt Dirks, Debbie Gowensmith, Jim Hawley, and Helen Turnbull
Editor: Karl Leuthauser
Creative Development Editor: Dave Thornton
Chief Creative Officer: Joani Schultz
Copy Editor: Betty Taylor
Art Director: Ray Tollison
Computer Graphic Artist: Nighthawk Design
Production Manager: Michelle M. Kucharski
Cover Art Director: Jeff A. Storm
Cover Designer: Jeff A. Storm
Cover Illustrator: Joe Sorren
Illustrator: Matt Wood

Unless otherwise noted, Scripture taken from the HOLY BIBLE, NEW INTERNATIONAL VERSION®. Copyright © 1973, 1978, 1984 by International Bible Society. Used by permission of Zondervan Publishing House. All rights reserved.

Library of Congress Cataloging-in-Publication Data
Understanding God together : 13 Bible studies for youth ministry.
    p.   cm.
   ISBN 0-7644-2101-8
   1. God--Biblical teaching--Study and teaching. 2. Bible--Study and teaching. 3. Church group work with teenagers. 4. Christian education of teenagers. I. Group Publishing.
BS544.U53 1999
268'.433--dc21   98-45113
                                                                   CIP

10 9 8 7 6 5 4 3 2 1   08 07 06 05 04 03 02 01 00 99
Printed in the United States of America.

"My purpose is that they may be encouraged in heart and united in love, so that they may have the full riches of complete understanding, in order that they may know the mystery of God, namely, Christ, in whom are hidden all the treasures of wisdom and knowledge."

—Colossians 2:2-3

Contents

Introduction .5

The Lessons

1. God is **loving.** 8
2. God is **forgiving.** 17
3. God is **holy.** 24
4. God is **powerful.** 31
5. God is **personal.** 38
6. God is **just.** 44
7. God is **compassionate.** 52
8. God is **our Father.** 58
9. God is **faithful.** 67
10. God is **generous.** 75
11. God is **merciful.** 85
12. God is **majestic.** 93
13. God is **sovereign.** 102

Introduction

"We use curriculum in our youth ministry. We just have to adapt so much of it. Sometimes I wonder if it would be quicker to do it ourselves."

"I bet that idea would work great for other churches. But we have one youth group with younger *and* older students. It just wouldn't work at my church."

Junior high and senior high kids differ from each other. They have different levels of maturity and different problems. Your junior high kids might be terrified of beginning high school while your senior high students may be dying to get out. But that doesn't mean you have to separate them to reach them.

By concentrating on the areas that *everyone* can grow in—the knowledge, understanding, and appreciation of God—*Understanding God Together* reaches youth of *all* age levels in profound and personal ways. By looking at the eternal mystery of who God is and how this mystery affects our lives, this book provides an entry point for all teenagers—regardless of their maturity in Christ.

Each lesson starts with an unmistakable aspect of God's character. It helps teenagers see who God is as revealed in the Bible. The lesson then demonstrates the implication that the attribute has for our lives as Christians. For example, by learning that God is holy, teenagers will discover that they are called to a high standard. By searching God's faithfulness, students will find that they will never be alone. The lessons encourage teenagers to share their personal experiences and to explore their own feelings regarding God's attributes and their responses to who God is. From there, each lesson challenges teenagers to apply the principles to their own lives. Students will be encouraged to make personal commitments to change and to act on those commitments.

No matter where the teenagers in your group are in their relationships with God, this book will help them deepen those relationships.

As you teach the lessons in this book, keep in mind the following tips for fostering learning in multi-age groups:

- Encourage older students to challenge and mentor the younger ones. Help your older teenagers understand that they are responsible to model Christian behavior as well as to teach it because the younger students are watching them.
- Challenge younger students to outthink the older ones. Continually praise them for their maturity and insight.
- Set discussion ground rules that help younger students feel comfortable sharing their thoughts and feelings with the group. For example, you could use the following rules:
    - Only one person in each group should be talking at any given time.
    - You are welcome to disagree, but please don't argue or fight.
    - Never attack a person for his or her opinion.
    - Listen before you speak.
    - It's OK to say "I don't know."
    - If the leader changes plans or interrupts a discussion, be flexible.
- Set appropriate boundaries. For example, let your group know that it is not appropriate for a seventh-grade girl in your group to date a senior guy from your group. Carefully monitor the group to make certain that no one takes advantage of the vulnerable discussions that may take place.
- Help kids stay focused. A healthy group with mixed age levels can provide an excellent way to help younger teenagers pass into young adulthood and to help older teenagers understand their significance. As long as teenagers realize they are trying to help one another mature in Christ, a mixed-age group can provide a wonderful learning and training atmosphere.

"For who has known the mind of the Lord that he may instruct him?" But we have the mind of Christ.
1 Corinthians 2:16

Because God is loving,
God made the ultimate sacrifice for you.

Objectives

Through this lesson, students will
- hear a story of personal sacrifice,
- explore salvation in the book of Romans,
- role play life situations, and
- reflect on their relationship with God.

For this lesson, you'll need
- Bibles
- pencils
- scissors
- "The Gospel in a Book" handout (p. 15)
- "The Difference It Makes" handout (p. 16)

Understanding God's Love

Watch the evening news tonight, and you'll see stories about unspeakable human atrocity. But every so often, a story sneaks through about self-sacrifice and love. A person gives or risks his or her life to save a child or an elderly person. Often we don't know the people involved, but their courageous acts make us feel a kinship with the good they perform. And we all feel renewed by the potential for good in humankind.

Perhaps the notion of sacrifice—as the ultimate way to show love for another—makes us appreciate love more. Scripture recognizes the uniqueness of self-sacrifice in Romans 5:7: "Very rarely will anyone die for a righteous man..." But when we consider that "while we were still sinners, Christ died for us" (Romans 5:8), we can only conclude that God's love for humankind is the greatest expression of love that the world will ever know.

What great news for young people! They have an opportunity to respond to God's love now with the prospect of a full life ahead of them.

Getting Started

(10 minutes)

Read the following true story to your group.

> In the late 1930s, the German Nazi war machine conquered the country of Poland, among others. Heinrich Himmler, the head of Germany's notorious special police, or SS, chose a small industrialized town in south Poland for the largest crematorium in the world. The land was annexed in 1939, and the labor camp was named Auschwitz. In four years, four million people were executed—gassed, shot, tortured, and starved to death.
>
> In May 1941, Nazis arrested several Catholic priests for running a forbidden school. The Gestapo ignored the priests' protests that the school was for training priests and not for general education. The priests' leader, Father Kolbe, was granted permission to appoint his successors before he was taken to Auschwitz.
>
> When Father Kolbe and the four priests with him arrived at Auschwitz, it was both a labor camp and a death camp. Hundreds of thousands died because of the working conditions. Because of the bleak outlook for survival, escape attempts were common. Unfortunately, the prisoners left behind paid a terrible price when an escape was successful—random prisoners were selected to be killed.
>
> At the end of a hot July day, Father Kolbe and the block of men with him awaited the selection of those to pay the price for an escaped prisoner. At seven o'clock, two of the most notorious Gestapo officers, Fritzsch and Palitzsch, examined the rows of silent, fearful prisoners. The officers' hats carried the death's head insignia of the Gestapo, appropriate for the actions they were about to perform.
>
> The SS chose one man from each row of ten men. Those chosen were ordered to step forward. A Polish sergeant, Franciszek Gajowniczek, cried out in desperation, "My poor wife and children!"
>
> Suddenly, Father Kolbe, standing a few feet away from the condemned man, took several steps forward. Prisoners were shot for breaking rank, as Kolbe then did.
>
> But Fritzsch, who had never spoken to a prisoner, asked, "What does this Polish pig want? Who are you?"
>
> Kolbe said he was a Catholic priest and added, "I want to die for that man. I am old; he has a wife and children."
>
> Fritzsch, showing no emotion, changed a number on his list and ordered Gajowniczek to return to his place in line. Father Kolbe, along with the other condemned prisoners, was led away to Cell 18, where his last days would be spent. Father Kolbe took care of his dying flock, with prayer and the reciting of psalms.
>
> After two weeks of starvation in a concrete bunker, only four men were alive, and Father Kolbe was the only one conscious. The authorities ordered an officer from the hospital barracks to inject poison into the veins of the priest. At 12:05 p.m. on August 14, 1941, Father Kolbe died at the age of forty-seven.

Ask:
- What were your emotions as I read this story?
- What is your opinion of Father Kolbe's actions? Explain.
- Could you do what Father Kolbe did? Why or why not?
- How would you define "sacrifice"?

Say: **Father Kolbe gave up his life for someone he had known for only a few months. As wonderful as his sacrifice was, we're going to look at a sacrifice that surpasses Father Kolbe's. God made the ultimate sacrifice for you, and because he did, you can experience God's love in a life-changing way.**

God Is Loving
(15 minutes)

If you have three teenagers in your group, give them the first three sections of the handout (Sections 1, 2, and 3), and keep Section 4.

For Junior High Students

Some younger students may have difficulty answering the questions on the handout. The questions are designed to challenge kids' thinking about God's actions. It's OK if they struggle with the responses. If they come away with a sense of awe for God's love, they have grasped the meaning of the activity and questions.

Photocopy one "Gospel in a Book" handout (p. 15) for every two students, and cut apart the four sections. Have students form pairs.

Give Sections 1 and 2 to the first pair, Sections 3 and 4 to the second pair, and repeat the same pattern with additional pairs. Say: **The gospel of Jesus is explained in the book of Romans. Read the Bible passages and answer the questions on each card.**

Give pairs three minutes to study their cards and answer the questions. After three minutes, have the pairs who were given Section 1 read the passage and share their answers to the first question. Before moving to Section 2, ask if anyone has any questions. Repeat this process for each section. When all sections have been presented by the pairs, ask:
- **What part of the sections we've explored means the most to you? Why?**
- **God sacrificed his Son. What sacrifices do you need to make as a Christian?**
- **How do your sacrifices compare to God's?**

Say: **When we compare God's sacrifice to sacrifices we make, it is clear that God made the ultimate sacrifice for us. And when we consider how God helps us in our lives, the sacrifices we make to follow him are minimal. Let's explore the ways God helps us live as Christians.**

What That Means for You
(20 minutes)

Say: **When we accept the love and forgiveness of God, we begin a lifelong process of growing more like Christ. God continually forgives our sin, but he wants us to have a life that isn't run by sinfulness.**

Have kids form groups of three or four. Give each student a "Difference It Makes" handout (p. 16). Say: **In your groups, discuss difficult situations that you face in different areas of your life as shown on the handout. Choose one of the situations, and with your group, create a brief role-play. Before you create your role-play, have each group member share one difficult example he or she has faced.**

Give groups about ten minutes to prepare their role-plays. Then have each group perform one role-play. When each group has completed one role-play, have groups perform a second role-play, and so on, as time permits.

Ask:
- **What was it like to do the role-plays?**
- **How could this activity help you the next time you face a situation similar to the examples you role played?**
- **How does God's love help you live a life that is pleasing to him?**

Say: **Because God made the ultimate sacrifice for us, we can have lives filled with love for God and others. Let's see how God's love made a difference for the church and how it can make a difference for our lives as well.**

Living God's Truth
(10 minutes)

Read the following epilogue to the story about Father Kolbe.

In October 1982, the man who Father Kolbe died for witnessed the sainthood ceremony of Father Maximilian Kolbe led by Pope John Paul II.

The church reported, this "step is being taken for the good of the Church and to the benefit of the people of God. It is felt that it will be an effective 'sign' that this holy man is held up in this way as an example to the Church."

Say: **Father Kolbe sacrificed his life and was honored as a saint. But Jesus sacrificed his life to give the opportunity for eternal life to you and me. Think about your relationship with Jesus. Some of you may need to think about accepting the love God offers through the sacrifice of his Son, while others of you may need to think about your relationship with Jesus. Reflect on the following questions:**

- What does Jesus' sacrifice mean to you?
- How has Jesus' sacrifice made a difference in your life?
- If you haven't responded to God's love, how can Jesus' sacrifice make a difference in your life?

Give students a few minutes to reflect on their relationship with the Lord. Close with a prayer, thanking God for making the ultimate sacrifice for us.

Helping Youth Become Christians

To help students learn how to become Christians, you may seek the assistance of your church's pastor. Many Christians use the following model as the first steps to becoming a Christian:
- Admit that you are a sinner in need of forgiveness.
- Acknowledge that Jesus paid the price for your sins through his death.
- Ask God to forgive you for your sins.
- Tell God that you want him to take control of your life and that you give him control of your life.
- Thank God for forgiving you and making you his child.
- Tell someone about the steps you took and why you took them.
- Talk to your pastor about what it means to belong to a church.

To Follow Up

Have kids each prepare a several-paragraph account of their faith history. Have kids share their stories during a youth meeting or youth event at church. If possible, vary the type of experiences they share. For example, you could have one junior high and one high school student share one week, a new Christian and a more mature believer share another week, and so on.

To Follow Up

Have kids volunteer to perform a worship service at a local nursing home. Nursing homes usually have Sunday services, and the residents love to have kids come and be with them. You could have one teen explain his or her faith history and have others play a piano, lead singing, or serve the Lord's Supper. After the service, have the kids gather for lunch and to talk about how they shared the love of God in serving the residents.

To Follow Up

Organize an "I'll Sacrifice My Time Project." Put an insert in the church bulletin asking church members to write down ways the teens could serve them over a weekend. You may list standard items such as baby-sitting, lawn or garden care, simple car maintenance or cleaning, or household chores. Give church members a few weeks to come up with their needs, and hold the event over a weekend. Conclude the project with a fun Sunday evening meeting featuring pizza and a time to share experiences.

Bible Insight

Warren Wiersbe, in his *Bible Exposition Commentary,* offers an outline of chapters 1 through 8 of the book of Romans that effectively summarizes the gospel.

Section 1: Sin—1:18-3:20

    A. The Gentiles guilty—1:18-32

    B. The Jews guilty—2:1–3:8

    C. The whole world guilty—3:9-20

Section 2: Salvation—3:21-5:21

    A. Justification stated—3:21-31

    B. Justification illustrated in Abraham—4

    C. Justification explained in Adam—5

Section 3: Sanctification—6-8

    A. Victory over the flesh—6

    B. Liberty from the Law—7

    C. Security in the Spirit—8

This outline could be used to expand understanding of the "Gospel in a Book" activity.

About God's Love

Love's ultimate origin is found in God. It is a part of his nature. Therefore, any expression of love, whether God's or humankind's, comes from God. First John 4:8b ("God is love") points to the roots of love contained in the Godhead.

However, it was through God's revelation through biblical history that the concept of God's steadfast love was made apparent to his people. During the dark periods of Israel's decline and captivity, the prophets regularly reminded the people of God's steadfast love (Isaiah 63:7).

The Gospel in a Book

Instructions: Photocopy and cut apart the four sections.

Section 1: Our Condition

The gospel of Jesus is explained in the book of Romans. Read the Bible passages, and answer the following questions.
Read Romans 3:23; 6:23.
- How would you describe sin?
- Why do you think you sin?
- Why do you think death is the penalty for sin?

Section 2: God's Sacrifice

The gospel of Jesus is explained in the book of Romans. Read the Bible passage, and answer the following questions.
Read Romans 5:6-8.
- Why do you think God would require sacrifice for sin?
- What do you think about Christ's death for *you?*

Section 3: Our Opportunity

The gospel of Jesus is explained in the book of Romans. Read the Bible passage, and answer the following questions.
Read Romans 10:9-10.
- Why are your mouth and your heart important in being saved?
- Why do you think God offers salvation in this way?

Section 4: Our Blessings

The gospel of Jesus is explained in the book of Romans. Read the Bible passage, and answer the following questions.
Read Romans 5:9-11.
- How would you describe being justified?
- How is your life different because of Christ's life in you?

Permission to photocopy this handout from *Understanding God Together* granted for local church use.
Copyright © Group Publishing, Inc., P.O. Box 481, Loveland, CO 80539.

The Difference It Makes

Instructions: Discuss difficult situations from your life that relate to the following areas. Use the first set of questions to help you create role-plays of those experiences. Then use the questions at the bottom of the page to guide your discussions.

The Situations

1. How I relate to my friends

2. Getting along with my family

3. Relationships with the opposite sex

4. My school experience

5. My standards of purity

6. My relationship with God

Creating the Role-Play

- Who was important in the situation?
- What made the situation difficult for you?
- What actually happened in the situation?
- How did the situation turn out?
- Who helped you during your experience?

Discussion Questions

- How did you respond in the relationship or situation before being guided by God?
- How do you think God could have helped you?
- Did you make a Christian response in your situation? If yes, what did you learn?
- How was your response different because of Christ in your life?

Permission to photocopy this handout from *Understanding God Together* granted for local church use.
Copyright © Group Publishing, Inc., P.O. Box 481, Loveland, CO 80539.

Because God is forgiving,
God can set you free.

Objectives

Through this lesson, students will
- come to understand why they need God's forgiveness,
- talk about sins they struggle with,
- take real steps toward resisting sin, and
- commit to allowing God to set them free.

For this lesson, you'll need

- Bibles
- a bucket of playground sand
- baby wipes
- copies of the "Forgiveness?" handout (p. 22)
- newsprint
- markers
- copies of the "Sin-Tracking Chart" (p. 23)
- pens

Understanding God's Forgiveness

Sin is an addiction. It starts small. Maybe it's just a little habit that you picked up from hanging around your friends. Maybe it provides a much-needed release from the frustrations of the day. But it slowly grows. Oh, you're still in control—the little sin just provides a way through the circumstances. But as it grows, the sin consumes you. It warps the way you look at others, yourself, and God. You feed into it as it becomes more complicated and consuming. And it doesn't stop until you are emotionally, spiritually, and physically dead—unless you repent.

You just have to turn to Christ. That's all it takes. He forgives the sin, restores your relationship with God, and heals the way you feel about yourself. Jesus gives you the power to change, to seek reconciliation with others, and to live in complete victory. His forgiveness is complete and more powerful than any kind of therapy. And it's free to all of those who will humble themselves and ask for it.

Getting Started
(15 minutes)

> If you don't have enough students to make a tight circle, have kids join hands to form a circle around the person in the center or have a few adult volunteers help out.

Have kids form a circle. Ask a volunteer to stand in the middle of the circle. Have kids form a close and impenetrable circle around the person in the center. Once the impenetrable circle is in place, ask the person in the center to try to break out. Tell the student in the middle that he or she cannot use his or her arms to break free and cannot run or jump. The person in the middle must try to slowly push his or her way out of the circle. Carefully monitor the activity for safety. When the person in the center appears frustrated or has escaped, allow others to try this exercise. After everyone has had a turn in the middle, ask:

● **How did it feel to be trapped in the center?**
● **How did you feel once you were able to break through to the outside of the circle?**
● **How is being trapped in the circle similar to being trapped in sin? different?**

Say: **This exercise demonstrates the importance of God's forgiveness. Without God's forgiveness, we're trapped by the sins we commit. Without God, there is absolutely no escape from sin.**

Discuss the following questions with your students:
● **How does sin enslave us?**
● **How can you tell when you're enslaved by sin?**
● **What do you think happens to people when sin takes control of their lives?**

Say: **It's easy to feel trapped by our sin. However, once we're trapped, it's important to realize that God wants to set us free. It's good to remember that because we're sinful people, we'll do wrong, but it's essential to remember that when we do wrong, God desires to forgive us.**

God Is Forgiving
(15 minutes)

> **For Junior High Students**
>
> Sand has a tendency to spread easily. Help your younger students resist the urge to throw sand at others or to drop sand on the floor by causing this activity to move quickly and by keeping students focused on the purpose of the exercise.

Place a bucket of sand and a package of baby wipes in the middle of the room. Say: **In order to understand what sin is like, I'd like you to pass around this bucket of sand. When the bucket comes to you, I'd like you to take a handful of sand and rub it all over your hands. Try not to get any sand on the floor.**

Allow kids time to pass the bucket. When the sand has been passed around, ask:

- **How do your hands feel?**
- **How is the sand on your hands like sin? different?**

Say: **Our sin is a lot like this sand. It's dirty, it's abrasive, and we can't just shake it off. I'd like you to name one sin that this sand represents in your life.**

Allow time for volunteers to share their sins. After everyone has had a chance to share, ask kids to find a partner to shake hands with. Ask:

- **How does sand affect the way someone else's hands feel?**
- **How is that like how sin affects our relationships with others? with God?**

Say: **You can't shake all the sand off your hands. In the same way, you can never make your sins completely right.** Distribute baby wipes, and have students wipe their hands. Say: **God's forgiveness is like these baby wipes. God's forgiveness heals our relationship with him and others. It also makes us clean. After God forgives us, we are completely clean.**

Have students open their baby wipes and lay them in front of where they are sitting. Read Isaiah 53:1-6 aloud. Ask:

- **How are the baby wipes like Jesus? different?**

What That Means for You

(15 minutes)

Give each student a copy of the "Forgiveness?" handout (p. 22). Say: **Understanding God's forgiveness means that we have to understand our own sinfulness. Let's look at a real-life situation in which someone needed God's forgiveness.**

Have teenagers form two separate groups. Give groups time to read the story on their handouts. When everyone has finished reading, direct students to the questions at the bottom of the handout, and have students discuss the questions in their groups. When everyone has finished discussing, ask volunteers to share their answers. Then ask:

- **How could forgiveness have made a difference in Tim's situation?**
- **What does it mean to forgive someone?**

Say: **Sometimes it's difficult for us to forgive others. That's one difference between God's forgiveness and ours. Let's talk about some other differences.**

Have teenagers brainstorm the differences between our forgiveness and God's. Distribute newsprint and markers for kids to record their ideas. When groups have finished, ask them to share their ideas with the entire group. When everyone has shared, say: **The most important difference between God's forgiveness and ours is that our forgiveness does not cleanse sins. We need to forgive one another in order to live at peace. We need God's forgiveness in order to have our sins cleansed. God is the only one who can truly set us free from our sins.**

Living God's Truth
(10 minutes)

Give each student a "Sin-Tracking Chart" (p. 23) and a pen. Direct students to go to a secluded place. Say: **While forgiveness is a great thing, sometimes the sins that we need forgiven can be a bit personal. I'd like you to work through this handout on your own. Think about your life, and pick a few sins that get the best of you now and then.**

Give students a few minutes to complete their handouts. When everyone has finished or after about five minutes, say: **Please find a partner. Pick one sin, and report to your partner how you plan to deal with it.**

Give pairs time to discuss their sins. When pairs have finished, gather everyone together and ask:

● **How can we find freedom from our sins?**
● **What are some ways to deal with sins that we continue to struggle with?**
● **How would you define repentance?**

Say: **Once you repent of a sin, God completely forgives you. You become righteous, pure, and holy before God. He gives you the power to overcome or escape that sin in the future. While it may take some time before you see complete victory in that area of your life, God is able and willing to forgive and help you as long as you keep turning to him.**

Have students pray individually, asking God for forgiveness and help.

To Follow Up

To help your teenagers further explore God's forgiveness, consider going on a forgiveness retreat. Get away with your group, and give students time to work through private sin issues. During group times, teach about God's forgiveness and grace.

To Follow Up

Consider incorporating the theme of this study in an outreach event. Provide positive and fun activities such as volleyball or live music for teenagers in your community to enjoy. Rather than giving a talk or sermon, have a few students share their own experiences of God's forgiveness.

About God's Forgiveness

The great commentator Matthew Henry sheds light on the contrast between sin and God's forgiveness. Henry notes that because of God's forgiveness:

1. We must no longer live in sin, we must not be as we have been nor do as we have done.

2. The body of sin must be destroyed...we must get the vicious habits and inclinations weakened and destroyed; not only cast away the idols out of the sanctuary, but the idols of iniquity out of the heart.

3. We must be dead indeed unto sin...He that is dead is separated from his former company, converse, business, enjoyments, employments, is not what he was, does not what he did, has not what he had.

4. Sin must not reign in our mortal bodies that we should obey it. Though sin may remain as an outlaw, though it may oppress as a tyrant, yet let it not reign as a king. Let it not make laws, nor preside in councils, nor command the militia; let it not be uppermost in the soul, so that we should obey it.

Henry goes on to discuss the appropriate response to God's forgiveness:

1. We should walk in newness of life. "Newness of life supposes newness of heart, for out of the heart are the issues of life."

2. We should be alive unto God through Jesus Christ. "The love of God reigning in the heart is the life of the soul towards God."

3. We should yield ourselves to God, as those that are alive from the dead. "The very life and being of holiness lie in the dedication of ourselves to the Lord."

4. We should yield our members as instruments of righteousness to God. "The members of our bodies, when withdrawn from the service of sin, are not to lie idle, but to be made use of in the service of God."

Forgiveness?

Tim was having an awful day. To begin with, as he was driving to church, he was cut off. So Tim sped up to catch the people who were so rude to him. When Tim finally caught up with them, they rolled down their windows and started yelling at him. Tim couldn't believe that he was being insulted by people who were totally in the wrong.

After that, Tim went to the grocery store to pick up some chips for a party he was going to that night. He bought his groceries and went to his car. After Tim put the groceries in the car, he counted the change that the grocery clerk had given him. The clerk had shortchanged Tim three dollars. Normally he'd be nice and forgiving, but because of the rotten day he was having, Tim decided to go back and let her have it.

Tim didn't care how dumb he looked. Before he could forgive her, he needed to tell her off. People all over the store looked at Tim as he gave the clerk a rude lecture. The clerk denied that she had made a mistake and called her manager over. As Tim persisted, the clerk ran off crying.

- **Have you ever done something like this? Explain.**

- **Is it ever OK to withhold forgiveness? Why or why not?**

- **How would you have handled this situation?**

- **How do you think God would want Tim to handle this situation?**

Sin-Tracking Chart

A big sin area…	How it could ruin my relationship with God…	How I am going to resist it…

Because God is holy,
you are called to a high standard.

Objectives

Through this lesson, students will
- strive to do their best in various activities,
- experience God's holiness through a heavenly scene,
- compare God's holiness to their sinfulness, and
- commit to holy living.

For this lesson, you'll need

- Bibles
- newsprint
- tape
- markers
- yardstick or tape measure
- pens
- paper
- copies of the "High Standard Contest" handouts (p. 30)
- white poster board
- two clear glasses filled with water
- a small amount of dirt in a sandwich bag

Understanding God's Holiness

When you read the incredible throne-room scene recorded by the Apostle John in Revelation 4, you come away with an overwhelming sense of God's majesty. Jeweled thrones surrounded by rainbows. Majestic creatures with multiple eyes and wings. Multitudes praising God continuously.

When faced with the incredible holiness of God, it's apparent that we cannot of our own efforts reach his standard. How can we respond when we hear Jesus' words in the Sermon on the Mount: "Be perfect, therefore, as your heavenly Father is perfect" (Matthew 5:48)?

Holiness is found in God alone. However, it is our responsibility to strive to live according to God's standard. We are to take Jesus' admonition for perfection literally and seriously. We are to strive for perfection while acknowledging that our righteousness is found only in Jesus' death and forgiveness.

Getting Started

(15 minutes)

Before your meeting, use paper and markers to make three signs. Label the first sign "Physical," the second "Mental," and the last "Social."

Tape a six-foot sheet of newsprint vertically along a gymnasium or outside wall so that the top of the sheet is about eleven feet high. Place markers and a yardstick at the foot of the newsprint. Tape the "Physical" sign next to the six-foot sheet of newsprint. In another area of your meeting area, place enough Bibles for a third of your group and tape the "Mental" sign near them. Finally, tape the "Social" sign in another area of your meeting room.

Say: **Welcome to the High Standard Contest. Each of you will compete to reach a high standard in a physical-, mental-, and social-skills activity.**

Give each student one "High Standard Contest" handout (p. 30) and a pen. Have kids form three equal-size groups. Direct each group to one of the three areas. Give students a minute to read the description of each contest.

Say: **Each of you will have one minute to try to reach the high standard for your activity and record it on your handout. I'll signal when time's up. When I signal, move clockwise to the next activity. Are there any questions?**

Have kids begin. Give a signal for teenagers to move at one-minute intervals.

For Junior High Students

Junior high students probably won't be able to perform as well as high school students. Make sure you address this during the debriefing of the activity. The standards are specifically designed to be very difficult to reach.

After everyone has completed the challenge activities, have groups gather in a circle. Determine whether anyone reached the goal in the challenge areas. If someone did, ask him or her:

● **How did you reach the goal in the activity?**

Ask everyone:

● **What was it like, trying to reach the goals in this game?**
● **Were some challenge areas easier for you? Explain.**
● **What are some other areas in your life that require a high standard?**
● **How was this challenge like or unlike how you strive to reach high standards in these other areas?**

Say: **Our High Standards Contest was designed to be difficult. Your age, maturity, and abilities may have determined how well you did. There is a standard that is not affected by things like age and ability. God's standard for us depends entirely on our standing before him. Holiness is not determined by our physical, mental, or social skills. We can all learn to live holy lives as a loving response to God's holiness. God is holy, and because you belong to him, you are called to a high standard.**

God Is Holy
(15 minutes)

Say: **Think of something that is so amazing or wonderful that you can't even describe it. Turn to a partner, and do your best to describe your thoughts to him or her. Then switch roles with your partner.**

Give kids three minutes to share their thoughts. Ask:
- **Were you able to explain your thoughts to your partner? Explain.**
- **Were you able to understand your partner's description? Explain.**
- **What did you describe to your partner?**
- **Why did you choose this thing to describe?**

Say: **You described some amazing and wonderful experiences. The Apostle John also experienced something amazing and wonderful. He was able to see a vision of heaven.**

Give kids newsprint and markers.

Say: **As you hear John's description of heaven, imagine you're there with him, seeing these amazing sights. As I read, draw pictures or write words on your newsprint to describe what you're envisioning as you hear the description.**

Read Revelation 4:2-11 slowly, pausing fifteen to twenty seconds between each verse to allow kids time to draw the scene described. When kids have finished drawing the scenes, say: **Now that you have a collection of some of the images, take a few minutes to write a summary of your pictures and words.**

Give students a few minutes to summarize and display their drawings. Ask:
- **What emotions did you experience while drawing heaven?**
- **Why do you think the creatures never stopped saying, "Holy, holy, holy" to God?**
- **How does this picture of creatures praising God's holiness compare to your descriptions of an amazing or wonderful experience that you discussed earlier?**

Hold up a piece of white poster board, and say: **God's holiness is like the pure white of this poster board because it is whiter than anything else in this room. God's holiness is unlike this poster board because the poster board has small imperfections in it.** Have kids choose objects in your meeting area to use as illustrations of God's holiness. Once kids find their objects, have each student answer these questions:
- **How is God's holiness like your object?**
- **How is God's holiness unlike your object?**

Say: **God's holiness is so amazing and wonderful. The objects we chose really can't begin to properly describe it. Even the picture of heaven falls short of fully describing God's holiness.** Ask:

● **How does knowing we can't fully understand God's holiness make you feel? Why?**

Say: **Even though we can't fully understand God's holiness, we can know enough to respond by striving to live holy lives. Because God is holy, you are called to a high standard. Let's see how we can have a high standard of holiness in our lives.**

What That Means for You

(20 minutes)

You might want to have kids do this object lesson on their own. Have teenagers form pairs. Give each pair a glass of water and a cup of dirt, and lead pairs in the object lesson.

Prepare this object lesson before class. You'll need two clear glasses filled with water and a small amount of dirt in a sandwich bag.

Point to the two glasses of water. Say: **This water is clean, pure, and drinkable. At the moment we become Christians, our lives become like these glasses of water—they become useful, sparkling, and refreshing.**

Ask kids to list specific sins teenagers struggle with. When a sin is listed, drop a pinch of dirt into one of the glasses. Continue dropping pieces of dirt into the glass for each sin listed. After everyone has had a chance to list a sin, ask:

● **What words would you use to describe the water inside this glass? Explain.**

● **How does this glass compare to the first one?**

● **What observations can you make about the glasses and holiness?**

● **What is holiness?**

Have kids form three groups (a group can be one person), and number the groups from one to three. Give each group a Bible, a pen, and a sheet of newsprint. Assign each of the following verses to the appropriate group:

group 1 (1 Peter 1:13-16)

group 2 (1 Peter 2:1-5)

group 3 (1 Peter 2:9-12)

Write the following questions on a sheet of newsprint, and tape the sheet to the wall:

● How is the word "holy" used in this passage?

● What requirements does this passage give for holiness?

● How can this passage help you to live a holy life?

Say: **With your group, read your passage; then discuss the questions on the sheet of newsprint. When you've finished discussing the questions, create a definition of holiness.**

Give groups about five minutes to study their passages and write definitions. Have kids share their responses. Then say: **You are called to a high standard. Jesus has made us holy, and it's our responsibility to live according to what he has done for us. It pleases God for us to strive to meet his standard of holiness. Let's make a commitment to do that now.**

Living God's Truth
(10 minutes)

Have kids gather around the six-foot piece of newsprint used in the "Getting Started" activity. Place a marker at the foot of the newsprint.

Have kids sit quietly and reflect on their need for holiness in specific areas of their lives. When a student is prepared to make a commitment to strive for holiness, have him or her go up to the newsprint and write the commitment on the newsprint and sign his or her name. If a student wants to keep his or her commitment confidential, simply have this student sign his or her name. Join students in making a commitment. When students have written on the newsprint, say: **We have all made commitments to live holy lives. Let's thank God for his holiness and ask him for strength to live out our commitments.**

Allow volunteers to contribute to a closing prayer.

To Follow Up

Have kids make a list of their favorite TV shows. While kids are watching the shows, have them rank the shows from one to five on a "holiness scale." A "one" rating means the show doesn't demonstrate or encourage holy living at all. A "five" rating means the show demonstrates and encourages holiness. After one week of rating their favorite shows, have kids report on their findings and how their TV viewing habits could change based on what they observed.

To Follow Up

Have kids create a dramatic presentation of the throne room scene in Revelation 4. The drama could be used during a youth worship or another special event. Kids could make simple costumes and chant the words in verses 8b and 11. More elaborate stage decorating and costumes could also be used. Challenge the kids to reach a higher standard in honoring God through their presentation.

To Follow Up

Have kids choose partners to be holy-living encouragers. Kids could exchange phone numbers and make a commitment to pray for one another.

About God's Holiness

The Hebrew word used to describe God's holiness is *only* used to describe him. The word refers to God himself or to what has been sanctified by him. Its primary meaning is "God is holy," in that there is no holiness apart from God (see Exodus 15:11). Holiness is more than a simple attribute of God. It represents his essential nature.

In God's divine actions, holiness is seen as an expression of God's divine personality (see Isaiah 5:16; 6:3). This divine holiness sets God apart from angels (Job 4:17-18), from heathen gods (Exodus 15:11), and from humans (Ecclesiastes 5:2). God defines holiness. He is the source and embodiment of all that is holy.

The High Standard Contest

Instructions: This is a challenge in three areas of your personal development: physical, mental, and social. You will begin at one of the challenge areas, perform a task, and record your performance in the space provided. You will have one minute in each of the three areas. You will be told when to rotate to the second and third areas. Remember, do your best!

1. Physical

The Goal: 11 feet

The Challenge: Mark the highest spot you can reach on the newsprint by jumping up and marking the spot with the marker. You'll have one minute. Measure your best height, and write it here.

_____

2. Mental

The Goal: 1 Peter 1:3-12

The Challenge: Beginning with 1 Peter 1:3, memorize as much of 1 Peter as you can in one minute. Close your Bible, and write what you remember here.

_____
_____
_____

3. Social

The Goal: Complete information from four people.

The Challenge: Find out the names, addresses, names of all cousins, favorite school subjects, hobbies, biggest frustrations, and greatest strengths of four people. Write the information here. You have one minute.

_____
_____
_____
_____

Because God is powerful,
you don't have to be afraid.

Objectives

Through this lesson, students will
- learn how God's power can protect them,
- discuss things that they're afraid of,
- discover how the world's idea of power is faulty, and
- commit to trusting God's power when they're afraid.

For this lesson, you'll need

- Bibles
- newsprint
- markers
- tape
- a glass of water
- thin cardboard
- copies of the "Fear in the Real World" handout (p. 36)
- copies of the "I Will Not Fear!" handout (p. 37)

Understanding God's Power

Teenage violence, divorce, abuse, road rage, terrorism—the list goes on. There are plenty of things for your teenagers to be afraid of today. In a desperate grasp for security, kids may withdraw, act tough, or arm themselves. Unfortunately, none of these methods brings real safety and none really alleviates fear.

Help your kids see that there's another way. Remind your kids that God is willing and able to watch over them and protect them. Of course, the world remains a dangerous place. But your teenagers can rest in the fact that God is in complete control. God will help them through difficult times and protect them from circumstances that are too difficult to bear. God is powerful *and* he's loving. As God's children, we really have no reason to fear.

Getting Started
(15 minutes)

Before students arrive, write, "I'm afraid of..." on a sheet of newsprint, and tape it to a wall. After students arrive, say: **Today we're going to talk about our fears and God's power. We'll start by talking about our fears.** Tell your students about one fear that hampers your ability to do God's will. Then have each person in the group share one of his or her real fears. After each person has shared, have the person write his or her response on the "I'm afraid of..." newsprint.

> Encourage kids to get beyond phobias, such as an unreasonable fear of snakes or water, and to share fears that affect the way they live their lives, such as a fear of losing a loved one or failing in school.

Say: **Today we're going to talk about fear. We'll see that we really don't have to be afraid of anything because God is powerful. Fear can paralyze Christians so they don't obey God or become who God wants them to be. For example, God wants us to help the poor, but many people don't take action because they're afraid they can't make a difference. Let's look at the fears we listed to see how they could stop us from doing what God wants us to do.**

Distribute markers. Have kids think of ways the fears they listed on the newsprint could stop them from doing God's will, and have each person write one response next to his or her fear listed on the newsprint. For example, if a student wrote, "getting shot" on the newsprint, he or she could write, "It could stop me from talking with or reaching out to people who look like they're in gangs." Or if a student wrote, "losing my parents" on the newsprint, he or she could write, "It could cause me to miss out on enjoying the time I have with them" on the newsprint.

Discuss:
- **Tell the group about a time when you were paralyzed by fear.**
- **How do you usually respond to fear?**
- **What purpose does fear serve?**
- **Are there any positive aspects of fear?**
- **What's the best way to handle fear?**

Say: **One of the best remedies for fear is an understanding of who God is. God is in control of everything. He is all powerful. Bad things will happen to us while we live on earth. But no matter what happens, God will be with us and will take care of us.**

God Is Powerful
(20 minutes)

Hold up a glass of water in front of the group. Say: **If I turn this glass of water upside down, the water will spill out. But with a simple piece of cardboard, I can make the water defy gravity.**

Teacher Tip: Practice turning the glass upside down before the study. Try cardboard pieces of various thicknesses and different amounts of water to make sure the water and cardboard will make a seal. Make sure that the cup is level when you hold it upside down.

Place a thin piece of cardboard on the glass of water, and hold the cardboard firmly with your hand while turning the glass upside down. Make sure that the glass is level. The cardboard should stay in place after you remove your hand. Ask:

● **Who can tell me the power that is working here?**

● **If I asked you, could you draw me a diagram or write the scientific principle that's at work here?**

● **If you hadn't seen this experiment, would you have let me hold the inverted glass over your head? Explain.**

Say: **In a way, God's power is like the forces at work in this experiment. We can't see it. And until we experience God's protecting power, it's difficult to believe in it. But once we've seen God's power in action, we trust it and realize that we don't have to be afraid. To strengthen one another's faith in God and in his protecting power, I'd like each of you to tell the group about a time when God protected you or someone you know.**

After each student has shared a story, say: **Look at the fear you wrote on the newsprint, and think about how God's power and protection relate to that fear.** Read Ephesians 3:20-21 aloud. Then have each person share with the group one way God's power and protection can help him or her through the fear.

What That Means for You

(10 minutes)

Have students form trios. Give each trio a copy of the "Fear in the Real World" handout (p. 36). Ask students to read the handout, discuss the questions on the handout, and then decide what advice they'd give to Bill and Jan concerning their fears.

When students have finished, have each trio share what it decided it would say to Bill and Jan. As a group, discuss:

● **How could God's power help Bill and Jan?**

● **Describe a time when one of your fears came true.**

● **What emotions surrounded the event?**

● **How did you feel about God?**

Ask a volunteer to read Romans 8:38-39 aloud. Say: **Even though God is powerful, bad things still happen. We all go through difficult times in life. But we don't have to be afraid of them. No matter what happens, God is with us and he will help us through difficult times. Nothing can separate us from God and his love.**

Living God's Truth

(10 minutes)

Say: **Fear often results from a lack of trust. Whatever we're afraid of, we have to make a decision to trust God. Trusting God may not necessarily change our circumstances, but it will change the way we respond to and feel about the circumstances.**

Give each student an "I Will Not Fear!" handout (p. 37). Direct students to fill out the handouts. When kids have finished, ask volunteers to share their answers.

Say: **When you feel afraid, remember the acrostic that is on your handout. One of the best ways to handle fear is by remembering to First Experience the Almighty's Reassurance. When you feel afraid, look to God for his help and support.**

Close your meeting with a group prayer. Encourage kids to mention things to God that they're afraid of and ask God for his reassurance and protection.

To Follow Up

- Establish a "No Fear" policy with your group. Encourage your group to openly discuss their fears with their Christian friends. Have kids pray for one another and encourage one another to overcome their fears.

To Follow Up

- To help your kids understand the idea of power, take them on a field trip to a local power company. Ask a representative to explain the process of making power. You could also ask a science teacher to volunteer time to teach your group about the concept of power. Afterward have teenagers discuss the similarities and differences they see between God's power and the type of power you investigated.

To Follow Up

- Invite an elderly member of your congregation to share his or her personal experiences of God's power and faithfulness.

About God's Power

Consider these aspects of power and fear:

1. While God could wield his power freely, many times he chooses to use it privately. Sometimes God chooses to make his power known in moments that seem insignificant.

2. We don't always have a clear idea of when or how God is working. Sometimes we have no idea that we need God's power and therefore are oblivious when he uses his power for our benefit.

3. The combination of God's power and our fear can sometimes produce a moment when God works for our benefit with support and love. Without our need, God would not demonstrate his power. And without God's power, we'd have no hope.

Use these thoughts to supplement your study on power and fear. As you teach, help teenagers understand that they can take God at his Word. When God says that there's no reason to fear, he means it!

Fear in the Real World

Situation 1

Bill has been trying to get into the right college since grade school. Ever since fifth grade, he's devoted most of his time to his studies, leaving little time for friends or other activities.

Bill applied to four colleges that he hoped would accept him. All of them turned him down. Not only does he feel depressed, Bill's starting to think that he's not going to realize his dream of going to the "right" college. He's afraid that he'll have to go to a college that is less than superior.

- **Is Bill's fear reasonable? Explain.**

- **How should Bill handle his fears?**

- **Read Psalm 27:1-3. How does this passage relate to Bill's circumstances?**

Imagine Bill confided in you about his fears and disappointments. If Bill were a Christian, what would you tell him? What would you tell Bill if he weren't a Christian?

Situation 2

Jan's parents seem to bicker about everything lately. When things are going well, they seem to be going really well. When things are going badly, they're almost unbearable. During the last fight, Jan's mother slammed the door as she left the house. Jan's mom came back after a few hours but hasn't spoken with Jan's father since. Jan is terrified that her parents are going to get a divorce, and she doesn't know what to do.

- **Is Jan's fear reasonable? Explain.**

- **How should Jan handle her fears?**

- **How does Psalm 27:1-3 relate to Jan's circumstances?**

Imagine Jan confided in you about her fears. If Jan were a Christian, what would you tell her? What would you tell Jan if she weren't a Christian?

Permission to photocopy this handout from *Understanding God Together* granted for local church use.
Copyright © Group Publishing, Inc., P.O. Box 481, Loveland, CO 80539.

I Will Not Fear!

When I feel afraid of something, I will respond by_____.

When I feel afraid I will not_____.

> **F**irst
> **E**xperience the
> **A**lmighty's
> **R**eassurance

"The Lord is my light and my salvation—whom shall I fear?
The Lord is the stronghold of my life—of whom shall I be afraid?"
—Psalm 27:1

Because God is personal,
you can have a relationship with God.

Objectives

Through this lesson, students will
- discuss barriers to their relationship with God,
- discover aspects of God's personality, and
- take a stand regarding their relationship with God.

For this lesson, you'll need

- Bibles
- masking tape
- paper
- pens
- newsprint
- markers
- wood blocks
- nails
- hammers

Understanding God's Friendship

It seems a little ridiculous—the God of the universe wants to have a relationship with us. Not only does God want to have a relationship with us, he wants it to be close and personal. Fortunately, regardless of how ridiculous it sounds, God has instigated the friendship and provided for it through the death of his Son.

Of course, when we come to understand who God really is, we fall in love with him and desire to obey and serve him. God wants us to worship, pray, talk with him, and study his Word so that we can *know* him. As our friendship with God grows, we find that we care more about the things God cares about. We find that we *want* to do the things God wants us to do. Our friendship with God takes time and effort. As we listen to God, share our prayers with him, and learn about his plans; we begin to understand what it means to have a personal relationship with the God of the universe.

Getting Started
(20 minutes)

Before the study, use masking tape to mark a line down the middle of your meeting room. As students arrive, give each person five sheets of paper and a pen. Say: **On each of the five sheets of paper you have, write down something you'd like to say to God or something you need to hear from him. For example, you could write, "I'm overwhelmed with school" on the first sheet and "I don't know what to do after high school" on the second.**

After kids fill out all of their sheets, have students put their sheets in separate stacks and write their names on the tops of the stacks. Have all the students except one stand on the line you taped to the floor. Have the other student stand behind the line. Say to the one who is behind the line: **God is on the other side of this line, and your goal is to get your prayers to him. The people standing on the line will do everything they can to stop your prayers from getting through while they stay on the line. You may not cross over the line, but you may crumple up your prayers to throw them over. You may also run back and forth along the line. Does anyone have any questions?**

Give each student an opportunity to throw his or her prayers across the line. Then discuss:
- **How did you feel as you were trying to get your prayers to God?**
- **What do the people standing on the line represent in your life?**
- **How hard do you work to get through the barriers between you and God? Explain.**

Say: **Since God is personal, you can have a relationship with him. God knows you personally and wants you to know him. There are many things that get between us and God, such as our sin and the distractions of this world. We need to work through these barriers just as we need to work through the barriers in other relationships.**

God Is Personal
(15 minutes)

| If you have fewer than four people in your group, have students explore more than one passage or explore one passage yourself. |

Hang newsprint in four locations in your meeting room. Write one of the following Scripture references on each sheet of newsprint: Psalm 29; Isaiah 57:15-19; 1 John 1:5-7; and 1 John 3:1-3. Have kids form four groups (a group can be one person), and assign one of the sheets of newsprint to each group.

Say: **In order to have a relationship with someone, you need to spend time getting to know that person. One of the best ways to get to know God is to learn what he says about himself in the Bible. With your group, I'd like you to look up the passage listed on your sheet of newsprint. Then on your newsprint, list everything the passage says about who God is and what he is like.**

Give groups about five minutes to work. Have each group present its sheet to the rest of the class. Then say: **Obviously, these sheets of newsprint don't completely explain what God is like. But from what you've seen today, I'd like you to pick one of the aspects of God's personality that you most identify with or that you like most about God. Go stand by the sheet of newsprint that lists that aspect.**

After everyone is standing by a sheet of newsprint, ask:
- What aspect did you pick?
- Why did you pick it?
- Are there any aspects of God that you're uncomfortable with? Explain.
- Together, what do all these sheets say about who God is?
- What important aspects of God aren't represented on this sheet?
- Does this exercise strengthen or weaken your desire to have a relationship with God?

Read John 15:13-16 aloud. Say: **God wants us to spend time getting to know him. As we come to know God more, we'll discover how wonderful it is to have a relationship with him. God has called us his friends, and as his friends, we can get to know him personally.**

What That Means for You
(15 minutes)

Make sure teenagers won't damage your floor as they do this activity. You may want to do this activity outside, just in case.

If you don't have enough wood to give each person two blocks, have kids form groups and give each group the supplies. You could also do the demonstration in front of the group as an object lesson.

Give each student a small block of wood and a marker. Say: **I want to show you a picture of the personal love God has for you. The block of wood you have represents you. Write "me" on the block.**

Give each student another small block of wood. Say: **This block of wood represents God. Write "God" on the block. I'd like you to demonstrate your relationship with God by making the two blocks stick together.**

Give each student two nails and a hammer. Say: **The nails are God's love. Without God's love, you cannot have a relationship with him. God's love was shown for you when Christ was nailed to the cross for your sins. Fasten your blocks together with the nails.** Allow kids to nail their blocks together.

Ask:
- **What other connections can you find between the blocks and your relationship with God?**
- **How do the blocks fail to show what your relationship with God is like?**

Read Romans 8:38-39 aloud. Say: **Nothing can separate you from God's love. Since you are God's child, God is always with you and he wants to have a close relationship with you. Your blocks may come apart some day, but God's love for you will never end.**

Living God's Truth
(15 minutes)

Say: **Once you decide to have a relationship with God, you've crossed a line into the most wonderful and personal relationship you can ever have. Since your relationship with God is so important, I'd like you to sit and think about it for a minute.**

Have kids think about the following questions:
- **Do you have a relationship with God?**
- **If so, what is it like?**
- **Do you want a deeper relationship with God?**
- **What can you do to have a deeper and more personal relationship with God?**

Have all the kids stand on the masking tape line you used in the "Getting Started" activity. Then say: **Do you have a relationship with God? If so, what is it like? I'd like you to make a public stand regarding your relationship with God. First, if you're sure that you have a relationship with God, place your wood blocks on the right side of the line. If you aren't currently interested in a relationship with God, place your blocks on the left side of the line. If you're interested but not sure about your relationship with God, place your blocks on the line.**

After kids place their blocks, say: **Those of you who put your blocks on the left side of the line, thank you for your honesty. You are always welcome in this group, and it's important for you to be here. I'd love to talk with you if you have any questions, issues, or concerns. Those of you who put your blocks on the right side of the line, congratulations on taking part in the most incredible, personal, and important relationship you could ever be in. I'd like to talk with the people who put their blocks on the line. Please stay after the meeting so we can talk a little more about what a relationship with God is all about.**

Close the meeting in prayer; then spend as much time as necessary helping students who put their blocks on the line understand what a relationship with God is about.

To Follow Up

At the close of the meeting, it's important to notice where kids placed their blocks. Address the three groups in the following ways:
- Students who put their blocks on the line need immediate follow-up. Make sure you talk with them at the end of the meeting *and* that you give them a follow-up call or visit in three or four days.
- Do not give up on students who put their blocks on the left side of the line. Make sure you demonstrate that they are welcome and important members of your group. Consider helping them come to understand who Christ really is by building a relationship with each of them.
- Students who put their blocks on the right side of the line need support and nurturing. When they are struggling with issues or their faith, you can remind these students of the public commitment they made and encourage them to keep working at their relationship with God.

To Follow Up

A great way to follow up this study is to take kids out on the street with a video camera. Give kids an afternoon to ask people to react to the phrase "God is personal." Have students videotape answers to this question and offer it to your pastor as a teaching tool in one of his or her Sunday school classes, or use it at the beginning of your next lesson as a reminder of the previous week's lesson.

To Follow Up

Make this study more meaningful by inviting kids to work on their own. Give them these words that relate to aspects of God's personality to get them started on a word study: majesty, greatness, glorious, face, unfailing. Students can use a concordance, Bible handbook, commentaries, or Bible dictionaries. Have students share their findings at your next meeting.

About God's Friendship

Our relationship with God is made possible only through the free gift of salvation through Jesus Christ. However, our friendship with God as described in John 15:12-17 requires mutual effort. As the *Expositors Bible Commentary* explains, "Jesus defined friendship in terms of obedience. Christian friendship is more than a casual acquaintance; it is a partnership of mutual esteem and affection...The friend is a confidant who shares the knowledge of his superior's purpose and voluntarily adopts it as his own."

God takes the initiative by calling us his friends. God does the work of restoration, forgiveness, and relationship. In response to that work, Christians must adopt God's plan and desires. As God's friends, we are to care about what God cares about and do what God wants us to do.

Because God is just,
God wants you to have integrity.

Objectives

Through this lesson, students will
- experience our justice system through a mock trial and compare it to God's justice,
- discover through God's Word why his justice requires our integrity, and
- testify about their own integrity.

For this lesson, you'll need

- Bibles
- newsprint
- tape
- marker
- copies of the "Just the Facts" handout (p. 51)
- a gavel (You can use a wooden mallet, meat tenderizer, or even a hammer.)

Understanding God's Justice

God's love may be difficult to fathom, but it's easy to accept. We can take comfort in knowing that, just as the prodigal son was welcomed with outstretched arms by his father, we will also be embraced by God no matter how far we've previously strayed from him.

The idea of a *loving* God is comforting to us, but the notion of a *just* God is another matter. Knowing that God will forgive us for any sin we confess to him, we're too comfortable with "cheap grace" to trouble ourselves with a God who demands perfection. It's difficult and frightening to accept the fact that God will demand and implement perfect justice as we go into eternity.

According to the Bible, however, God's love and justice go hand in hand. His greatest act of love—sending his Son to bear the burden of our sin—was in response to the requirements of his justice. As Romans 3:25b says, "He did this to demonstrate his justice, because in his forbearance he had left the sins committed beforehand unpunished."

The way we view God makes a big difference in how we live our lives. When we properly fear God as the supreme judge of the world, we're much more likely to live with integrity. We are to respect God and forsake sinful actions. We must live with integrity while resting in the knowledge that perfection comes only through the price Christ has paid.

Getting Started

(10 minutes)

Have students form pairs. Instruct each pair to read Proverbs 11:19-21 aloud, with one person reading the first half of each verse and the other partner reading the second half. After pairs have finished reading, have them discuss the following questions:

● **What differences between righteousness and wickedness does this passage demonstrate?**
● **How would you define righteousness? wickedness?**
● **Who is the most righteous person you know?**
● **What makes that person righteous?**

After each pair has finished discussing the questions, bring the group back together. Tape a sheet of newsprint to the wall, and draw a vertical line down the middle of the sheet. On one side of the line, write, "Wicked People..." On the other side, write, "Righteous People..." Ask the students to show the difference between wicked people and righteous people by calling out characteristics or tendencies of both types of people. For example, a student could say, "A wicked person thinks only about himself," or "A righteous person puts her trust in Jesus." As students share, write their responses under the appropriate heading on the newsprint.

Ask:
● **How does integrity fit into this list?**
● **How does God's justice apply to this list?**
● **What's the main difference between righteousness and wickedness?**
● **How do you think God feels about each of the characteristics and tendencies we listed?**
● **How do you think God feels about the people who display these characteristics and tendencies?**

Say: **Wickedness can be defined as falling short of God's perfection. God, of course, wants us to live as righteously as we can. Since God is just, he does not close his eyes to any sin or wicked deed. We must strive to live righteously while remembering that God's perfect justice can be satisfied only through faith in Jesus. Let's take a closer look at righteousness, wickedness, and God's justice.**

God Is Just

(20 minutes)

Set up the room like a courtroom. Put the judge's chair and table at the front of the room and two tables with chairs facing the judge. These will be for the prosecution and defense teams.

Have kids form two teams, and tell students that they're going to participate in a trial. Say: **Joe Smith, a freshman in high school, has just been charged with destruction of property. He's accused of vandalizing Sam's Supermarket with spray paint. Your job is to prove whether or not he's guilty.**

Have one team play the part of the prosecution and the other team act as the defense. Give each team a "Just the Facts" handout (p. 51). Tell teams to use the facts on their handouts to prepare closing arguments for the trial. Instruct students to prepare their arguments as a team and select one person to present the arguments.

Give each team five to ten minutes to prepare its arguments. Then sit on the judge's bench, pound the gavel, and say: **Court is in session, the honorable** [your name] **presiding. The prosecution may start with its arguments.**

When the prosecution has presented its arguments, say: **The defense may now proceed with its arguments.**

When the defense attorney has finished, make a decision on the case. Explain which parts of each team's arguments sounded convincing to you, and issue your verdict. Read Isaiah 65:6-7 aloud. Then ask the students:

- **What punishment do you think the defendant deserves if he is guilty?**
- **Do you think criminals usually get what they deserve? Why or why not?**
- **Do you believe our legal system encourages people to live with integrity? Explain.**
- **What sentence do you think God would give Joe?**

Say: **Many of you have a strong sense of justice. But God's sense of justice is much stronger. God requires complete purity and integrity from us because God is completely pure. As Christians, we must try to live with integrity and to meet God's standards of purity. Fortunately, God knows that we will slip up from time to time. So God paid the penalty for our sins by sending his own Son to die for us.**

What That Means for You
(15 minutes)

Have teenagers form a circle. Ask:
- **Why should we strive to live with integrity when we can never live up to God's standard?**
- **Why should we avoid sinning when Jesus has paid for all our sins anyway?**

Say: **There are many reasons God wants us to live with integrity. Let's explore some of those reasons by telling a story together. Our story will be about a person who lives with integrity and a person who has no integrity. I'll start telling the story; then we'll go around the circle, and each person will add another few sentences to the story. When it's your turn, just think of a way to continue the story. As you tell it, try to demonstrate either the integrity of the one character or the lack of integrity of the other character. To begin, we need to decide what kind of story it will be. Would you like to tell a western, science fiction, detective, or romance story?**

Have the students vote on which genre the story will be. Depending on their decision, start the story with one of the following introductions, and then "pass" the story to the next person in the circle:

Western

In the lonely desert of New Mexico, one hundred miles from the nearest city, was the little town of Cactus Flats. It was a friendly town, a place where everyone knew everybody. Sheriff William T. Justice kept things in order just fine. That is, until the day Six-Gun Billy rode into town.

Science Fiction

"Blue six, I'm approaching the asteroid belt right now." Dash Jordan, the galaxy's finest fighter pilot, was on a crucial mission. An intergalactic thermonuclear detonator had been placed somewhere on Earth. He had to find the code that would de-arm it. To find the code, he set out to find the man who had planted the detonator, the evil Apollo Zeron. Apollo's hide-out in the asteroid belt came up on Dash's radar. He was about to come face to face with the most despicable man in the galaxy.

Detective

It was the crime of the century. On Thursday, $200 million in cash was sitting in the vault at First National Bank. The next morning, it wasn't. Detective Frank Spade knew that his job depended on this case. The only clue he had was a scrap of paper left at the bank with the word "Pops" written on it. Could it be Pops McGregor, the notorious international thief? There was only one way to find out.

Romance

As Tony leaned over the rail of the riverboat, he could see her on the deck below. Violet was more stunning than any woman he had ever seen in his life. But standing next to her was the one person who could keep them from a lifetime together—her father, Mr. Ritchie. As a wealthy and ruthless businessman, he had already made it clear to Tony that his daughter would never be allowed to speak to a lowly coal miner. They had only two hundred miles to go until the boat docked in St. Louis. And Tony was desperate to find a way past Mr. Ritchie to his true love, Violet.

Teacher Tip: Before starting the story, it might be helpful to remind kids to keep the story wholesome. If the students choose to create a romance story, you might want to remind them of their responsibility to avoid coarse jesting or any other objectionable behavior.

Let the story go around the circle a few times; then end the story. If time permits, allow the group to tell a few more stories. After the students have finished a story, ask:

● **How did our story demonstrate the difference between people who have integrity and people who don't?**

- Why is it important to have integrity?
- How do you think God's justice would apply to the hero? the villain?

Say: **The way we choose to live our lives affects the way others feel about us, the way we feel about ourselves, and the way we feel about God. No matter what others do, we need to keep God's justice in mind and try to live up to his standard. God knows that we can't be completely righteous, but God is pleased when we try to live our lives with integrity.**

Living God's Truth
(10 minutes)

Have students return to the pairs they formed in the "Getting Started" activity. Say: **In a trial, lawyers often bring in character witnesses to tell about a defendant's behavior and attitude. Each of you is now a character witness. I'd like you to testify about someone's character traits, both good and bad. But this is the catch: That someone is you. You're a character witness at your own trial. For example, you could say, "Jenny has accepted Jesus Christ as her Savior, and she is a loving, kind, and generous person. But she also has the tendency to lie sometimes by exaggerating the truth, and she often gets mad at her parents."**

Tell the pairs that after one student has testified, the other partner should help the person grow in integrity by praying for him or her. Encourage kids to thank God for strengths the person has testified about and to ask God's help in changing the areas of weakness.

For Junior High Students

To help students become comfortable with sharing their good and bad points, begin the activity by giving a truthful testimony about yourself. Share strong and weak characteristics about yourself. Be as open and honest as possible, and kids will see that it is good to be vulnerable with one another.

After both partners have testified, say: **You must decide what punishment you deserve according to the laws of our country and according to God's laws.** Begin by sentencing yourself for some of the ways you have sinned against God.

After all the students have sentenced themselves, say: **God's justice requires that all of us die for the sins we've committed. We deserve a life sentence in God's jail—without the possibility of parole.**

God's justice also means that he can't just wipe out our sins and forget all about them. They must be punished. That's why Jesus Christ came to pay the penalty for our sins. We all deserve death, but God has given us forgiveness and life. The penalty has been paid by Christ, and we have been declared innocent. However, that doesn't give us license to sin just because we know we'll be forgiven. God commands us to live with integrity even though we know our sins will be forgiven.

To Follow Up

Visit a local courthouse with your group. Call before you visit to get a schedule of criminal trials that are open to the public. You might want to exercise caution in deciding which types of trials to observe. While a homicide or assault trial might be too grisly for your students, a robbery or similar trial may be appropriate. Regardless of the type of trial you observe, make certain you have parental permission beforehand.

After you have observed all or part of the trial, ask students the following questions:
- **What is your general impression of the trial?**
- **Do you think the defendant is guilty? Explain.**
- **What sentence does the defendant deserve? Explain.**
- **How does the legal system compare to God's justice?**

To Follow Up

Set aside an evening to watch a popular TV sitcom or drama together as a group at someone's house, and assign your kids to take notes on each character. Have them note every time a character shows integrity and every time a character demonstrates a lack of integrity. Challenge your students to evaluate what television teaches about integrity.

To Follow Up

Develop a system of peer accountability among the students in your group that will challenge them to live their daily lives with integrity. Perhaps you can have the students commit to calling their partners (preferably same-sex) once a week for six months. Encourage partners to ask each other questions about their relationship with God, to pray for each other, and to encourage each other during tough times. Think of a creative name for these pairs, such as "Tag Teams" or "27:17 Groups" (referring to Proverbs 27:17).

About God's Justice

Many people perceive a difference between the angry, wrathful God of the Old Testament and the merciful, forgiving God of the New Testament. In reality, though, God's justice has not been diminished in any way. It has merely been postponed. According to 2 Peter 3:9, God is patiently withholding off his judgment as long as possible, "not wanting anyone to perish, but everyone to come to repentance." God desires every person to come to him, but will not fail to send his fury on any who refuse his invitation.

In his book *Knowing God,* J.I. Packer gives four characteristics that make up a judge. A judge is a person with authority, a person who is identified with what is good and right, a person of wisdom to discern truth, and a person of power to execute a sentence. God is the supreme authority of this world, both the lawgiver and the judge. He is the perfect fulfillment of goodness and righteousness. He knows us and judges us as we really are through his wisdom and omniscience.

Through his love, God has provided a way to stand under this judgment. God sent his Son to pay our penalty. Thus, God's justice is satisfied through his own mercy.

Just the Facts

Use this sheet as a guide to help you prepare your arguments. Select the facts that help support your position, and think of ways to explain away the facts that don't support your position.

POLICE REPORT

Defendant: Joe Smith   **Age:** 14

Alleged Crime(s): Destruction of property (vandalism with spray paint)

Location: Rear wall of Sam's Supermarket, 8274 North Maple Street

Time: January 24, 4:30 p.m.

Facts pointing to the defendant's guilt:
- The defendant was spotted by the store manager in the supermarket that day.
- When the defendant was questioned at home, a can of spray paint was seen on his front porch. The can contained paint that appeared to be the same color as the graffiti.
- Amid the graffiti were the letters "J.S.," possibly standing for "Joe Smith."

Facts pointing to the defendant's innocence:
- The defendant's best friend says that the defendant was at his house when the crime was committed.
- The can of spray paint seen on the defendant's porch was never tested to determine whether it was the same paint as the graffiti.
- At the same time the defendant was being questioned by police, a wall three blocks away was spray painted with the letters "J.S."

Because God is compassionate,
God wants you to reach out to those who are hurting.

Objectives

Through this lesson, students will
- learn that hurting people have identities and names,
- learn how important real solutions are when reaching out to the oppressed, and
- make a commitment to be people who reach out to hurting people.

For this lesson, you'll need
- Bibles
- baby name books
- paper
- pens
- copies of the "Band-Aid Solutions" handout (p. 57)
- newsprint
- tape
- markers
- cloth Band-Aids

Understanding God's Compassion

Stop! Before you read this, go look in the neighborhood around your church. Go ahead, I'll wait.

Glad you're back. Here are some things you may have seen:

- A homeless person searching through your church trash bin, looking for a meal.
- A single parent in a car at the stoplight. Her kids are acting up, and she's having a tough time disciplining them.
- An older woman attempting to climb a flight of stairs while carrying her groceries. You can tell by watching her that each step requires tremendous effort.

These are scenes your kids probably see every day. In fact, they see them so often they become numb to the fact that people in your community are hurting, broken, and desperately in need of God's comfort. Many people who face difficult circumstances triumph with dignity and pride. But there are people all around you who just can't seem to make it.

You and your students can make a difference. Use this study to challenge your group to really *see* hurting people and to *do* something about it.

Getting Started

(10 minutes)

Set out books that list names and explain their meanings. As students arrive, have each look up his or her name in one of the books. Give each student a sheet of paper and a pen. Say: **Think about how your name has influenced who you are. Imagine that you have a name other than the one you've been given. Write down that name, and then write a few sentences that describe how your life would be different with that name. For example, if you had been named Dumbo, maybe you would be more fun to be around but a little worse at schoolwork.**

For Your Students

If you don't own any name books, consider borrowing some from a few couples who are expecting babies, or borrow the books from a library.

Have students share what their real names mean, their pretend names, and how the pretend names could have changed their lives. Then ask:
- **Do you think names are important? Why or why not?**
- **Do names shape who we become? Explain.**
- **What would your life be like if you didn't have a name?**
- **What does it look like to treat a person like he or she doesn't have a name?**

Say: **Today we're going to learn more about God's compassion. We're going to see that God wants us to reach out to the hurting. Sometimes we forget that the hurting people we see or meet have names, personalities, or families. We get so accustomed to seeing hurting people that we forget to reach out to them with God's compassion.**

God Is Compassionate

(15 minutes)

Say: **Let's take some time to look at how God views hurting people.**

Have kids form pairs. Have a volunteer read Mark 2:1-12 aloud. Distribute Bibles; then say: **Imagine that Jesus has to take a break when the paralytic is lowered through the roof and you mistakenly sit in Jesus' chair. You and the paralytic ask after Jesus' whereabouts and find that he won't be back for thirty minutes. With pain in his eyes, the paralytic asks you, "Can you please help me?" With your partner, talk about what you would do. Prepare to retell the story to the group using this scenario.**

Have each pair tell its story. Then ask:
- **What could you give the paralytic?**
- **What couldn't you give?**
- **Imagine that Jesus walks back into the room as you are finishing your time with the paralytic. What would you want him to see?**
- **How can we follow Jesus' example of compassion in our daily lives?**

Say: **God's compassion is evident in the Bible. He helps, loves, forgives, and heals hurting people time and time again. While we can't match Jesus' power and compassion, we are his representatives to a hurting world. We need to follow Jesus' example and reach out to hurting people.**

What That Means for You
(15 minutes)

For Your Kids
It's easy for your kids to get bogged down in trying to name everyone in your community who *might* need help. It's just as easy to mentally check out of this activity because the problem might feel too big. To help kids keep a proper focus, have them list people who they can personally reach out to.

Say: **One way we try to deal with our feelings when we see someone who needs help is by doing something that doesn't take much effort. For example, when we see someone who's been abused by his or her spouse, we might offer a crisis hot line phone number. Taking action like this is not wrong in any way. But we need to follow Jesus' example. He did more than heal the paralytic. He forgave the paralytic's sins. In the same way, it's important for us to do everything we can safely do when it comes to showing God's compassion to others.**

Give each student a copy of the "Band-Aid Solutions" handout (p. 57) and a pen. Have individuals work through the first section of the handout as they think about people who need God's compassion. While students work, tape a sheet of newsprint to a wall.

When students have finished working, have volunteers report their results. As students report, write down their answers on the newsprint.

Say: **You've done a great job of identifying people who need God's compassion. Now find a partner to discuss the surface help or "Band-Aid" solutions we might offer to these people without really meeting their needs. Write your solutions in the middle part of your handout.**

Have pairs share their lists. Then say: **To successfully show God's compassion, you must understand the people who need it and you must seriously think and pray about how you can help. Let's work at finding real solutions for meeting real needs.**

Have pairs work together on the final section of their handouts. While students work, tape another sheet of newsprint to the wall and write, "Real Solutions" at the top of it. When pairs have finished, gather everyone together. Have students share their real solutions while you write each solution on the newsprint. When students have finished sharing, ask:

● **What differences do you see between the Band-Aid and the real solutions?**

● **How many of these ideas could you really put into practice? would you be willing to put into practice?**

● **How would you feel if someone tried to help you in these ways?**

Say: **If we're looking for opportunities and are armed with real solutions, God can use us to help those who are hurting. God is compassionate, and he wants us to reach out to hurting people. We don't have to feel guilty, and we shouldn't react impulsively. We should simply consider how we can show God's compassion to a hurting world and do it.**

Living God's Truth

(10 minutes)

Have a volunteer read Isaiah 58:6-12 aloud. Say: **God makes a promise to us. If we'll respond to his call and reach out to others with his compassion, he will meet our needs and bless us. God's promise is dependent on our action. We have to be willing to respond with God's compassion when we see people who are hurting.**

Distribute cloth Band-Aids and markers. Say: **I'd like you to commit to being a person who reaches out to hurting people.** Ask students to write on their Band-Aids one way they plan to reach out to hurting people. Close the meeting by asking God to help your kids notice hurting people and to be ready to act with his compassion.

As students leave, encourage them to stick their Band-Aids on their hands as reminders.

To Follow Up

Consider having your kids create a servant team. Have interested kids meet at a fast-food restaurant to plan a service project. Have the team divide responsibilities such as transportation, scheduling, supplies, and finances. If the team has difficulty coming up with a service idea, encourage kids to make a plan for volunteering at an organization or group that is actively involved in demonstrating God's compassion.

To Follow Up

Start a "Youth Ministry Minute" program at your church. Ask the senior pastor of your church for some time during the worship service. Invite one or more students to read Isaiah 58:6-12 and give a two-minute devotional on compassion. Consider having different students lead the Youth Ministry Minute every month.

To Follow Up

Help your kids gain a deeper understanding of compassion by taking them to various areas in your community where the need for compassion is evident. For example...
- go to a soup kitchen and offer to help serve.
- visit a crisis-pregnancy center, and arrange for interviews with teenage parents.
- arrange for your kids to deliver meals to people who are elderly or disabled.
- begin a compassion fund. Encourage your kids to bring pocket change to your meetings and then donate the money to a reputable charitable organization.

About God's Compassion

Isaiah's memorable words in chapter 58 strike a chord with people who are called to a life of serving oppressed people. In Old Testament times, fasting and giving to the poor were connected by law. Some also believed that these two activities were "the wings of prayer." God's support was available to those who did his work.

Isaiah's words are echoed by Jesus in Matthew 25:35-36. As Jesus spent time with his disciples, he demonstrated that serving others is part of being one of his followers. Jesus just wants us to serve.

If we bear the name of Christ, reaching out to hurting people ought to be part of who we are rather than a compartmentalized activity we do to make ourselves feel better. By reaching out to the oppressed, we fulfill God's call and serve Christ himself.

Band-Aid Solutions

Who are some of the people in your school, church, or community who need God's compassion?

What are some "Band-Aid" solutions to their hurts and pains?

How can you really reach out to their hurts and pains with God's compassion?

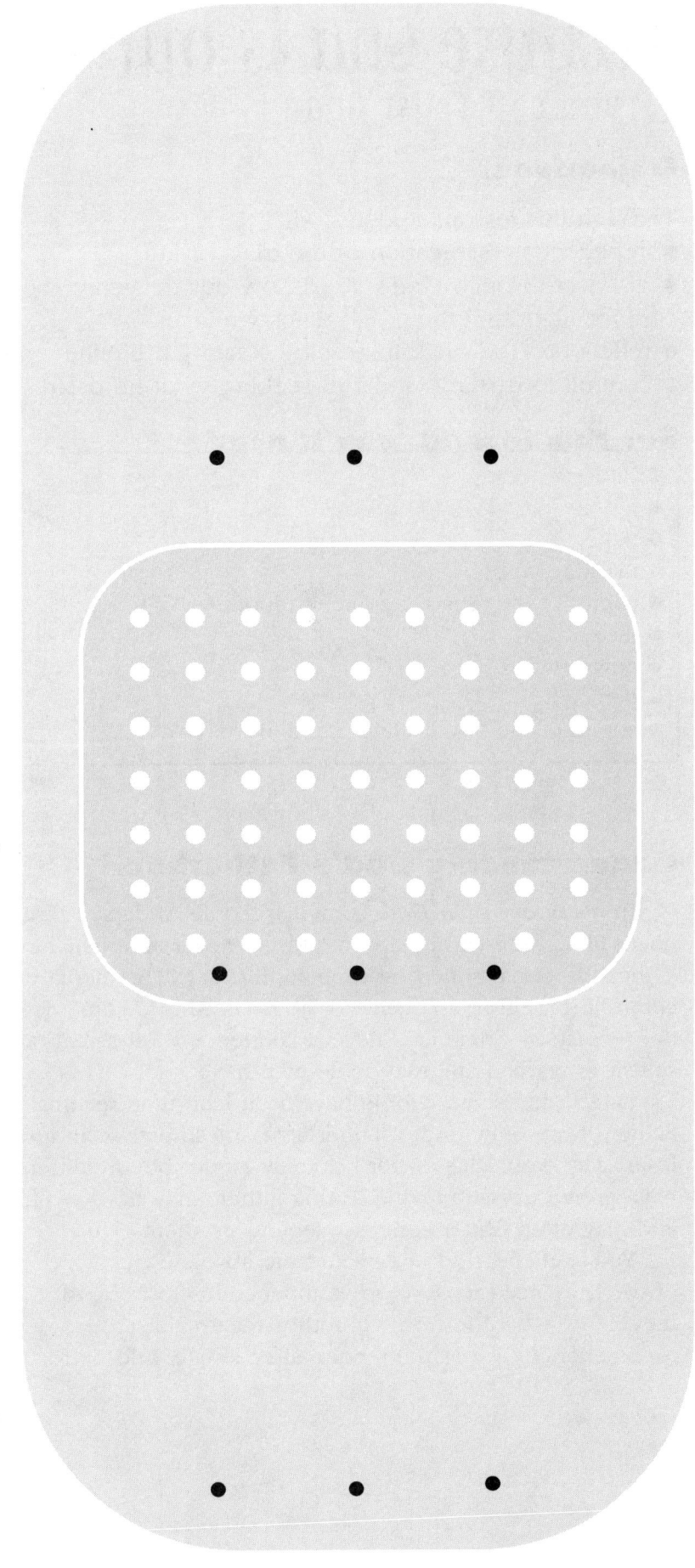

Handout

Permission to photocopy this handout from *Understanding God Together* granted for local church use.
Copyright © Group Publishing, Inc., P.O. Box 481, Loveland, CO 80539.

Because God is our Father,
you can trust God.

Objectives

Through this lesson, students will
- experience a simulation of the trials of life,
- discover through God's Word how our heavenly Father can be trusted to care for us during the tough times we face,
- reflect on God's faithfulness by creating a lifeline, and
- commit to trusting God and seeking what he desires.

For this lesson, you'll need

- Bibles
- a box
- paper
- masking tape
- copies of the "Surviving Life" handout (p. 65)
- dice
- newsprint
- pens
- copies of the "My Lifeline" handout (p. 66)

Understanding God's Fatherhood

In his book, *Dear Dad,* comedian Louie Anderson tragically explains, "My dad never hit us...he carried a gun. Oh, he never shot us...he'd just go "Click-click!" Fathers don't have the best reputation today. The media often portray them as controlling, selfish, apathetic, or abusive. And to some extent, fathers have earned the reputation. Some kids never experience what a real father is because of the selfish or warped attitudes some men have.

As a result, some people have a difficult time relating to God as their eternal Father. If the only kind of father a person knows is an inconsistent, unreliable loser, why would his or her heavenly Father be any different? Even people who have grown up with loving, caring fathers may have a difficult time trusting God and may often find it easier to depend on themselves.

Your kids need to understand the absolute trust God requires from each one of us. They need to develop confidence in God's hand in life's little things so that they know where to turn when they face major crises. Most of all, teenagers need to experience God as the tender, affectionate, and perfect Father he is.

Getting Started
(20 minutes)

Before the lesson, set up a giant board game in your meeting room. Create a starting point at one end of the room by putting a large open box on the floor. Make a winding path through the room by taping fifteen to twenty sheets of paper to the floor, leading to a finishing point at the opposite end of the room. Make one copy of the "Surviving Life" handout (p. 65) for every three students. Cut the sections apart, shuffle them thoroughly, and stack them.

Have all the students stand inside the starting box. Say: **You are now pieces in a giant board game called "Surviving Life." Your goal is to make it alive through your school years. There will be setbacks and advances along the way. But no matter what happens, you'll have to keep on trying until you reach the end.**

Have each teenager roll a die and go forward as many spaces as the die indicates. When he or she goes to the space, give the person a card from the top of the deck. Have the student read it aloud and follow the instructions on the card. After each student has taken his or her first turn, have kids continue taking turns by taking a card, reading it, and following the instructions. If time permits, play until all of the students reach the ending point. Have students who finish first cheer on the ones who remain.

Teacher Tip

If you have more than five or six kids in your group, you might want to have the students pair up and play the game as partners to save time.

Ask:
- **How was this experience like real life? different?**
- **What similar situations have you faced in your own life?**
- **What kinds of things cause you to worry or stress?**
- **Is it easy or difficult for you to trust God when tough times come? Explain.**

Say: **God understands when you're going through tough times. And God cares what happens to you because he is your loving and perfect Father. God wants you to understand that he has things under control, and that as your loving Father, he will take care of you.**

God Is Our Father
(20 minutes)

Tape a sheet of newsprint to the wall. Have students form trios. Say: **There are millions of fathers on this planet. Some are good fathers, but others aren't so great. I want you to think of the qualities that a good father possesses. For example, a good father is interested and excited about what his children are doing, and a good father has a good reason when he gets upset with his children. As your group comes up with ideas, call them out and I'll write them on the newsprint.**

As the students list the qualities of a good father, write their ideas on the left side of the newsprint. After they have listed ten to twenty characteristics, say: **Now I want you to think of the ways that God, as our heavenly Father, fulfills each of these qualities. For example, a good father is interested in his children, and God is interested in everything about us—he even knows how many hairs are on our heads!**

Write down student responses next to the qualities listed. Then have students form two equal-sized groups. Give each group a sheet of paper and a pen. Direct one group to read Matthew 6:31-34 and the other group to read Matthew 7:7-11. Then have each group write down the answers to the following questions in response to its assigned passage:

- **What commands does Jesus give?**
- **Sum up the passage in one sentence.**
- **If you had only this passage of the Bible to go on, how would you describe God?**

Teacher Tip

When students discuss a list of questions, write the questions on a sheet of newsprint, and tape it to the wall so that each group can move through the questions at its own pace.

When the two groups have finished discussing the questions, bring them back together to share their answers. After both groups have shared, say: **We don't need to worry about anything in life because God promises to take care of us. God knows exactly what we need in life—even if we don't. And we can trust our Father to do what's best for us.**

What That Means for You

(15 minutes)

Give each student a sheet of newsprint and a pen. Say: **We've all experienced times in our lives when things go great. We've all also experienced times when things go wrong and God seems a million miles away. Every person in this room has a different story to tell about his or her experiences.**

Give each student a copy of the "My Lifeline" handout (p. 66). Say: **Tell your story by creating a lifeline that shows your whole life up to this point. You'll show the high points of your life—when you took a great vacation with your family or when your team won the league championship, for example. You'll also show the low points in your life—when you lost a best friend or when you realized you were acting selfishly, for example.**

Instruct students to set up their lifelines by drawing a heavy vertical line at their present age. For example, if a student is now thirteen, have him or her draw a dark line at the "13" mark on the handout.

Say: **You're ready now to start drawing your lifeline. Start by putting your pen at the zero mark—when you were born. I want you to think about your life and reflect on the good and bad times you've had. For a** positive experience in your life, you'll draw your lifeline above the middle line at the point that corresponds to your age at the time. For a negative experience, you'll draw your lifeline below the middle line. Complete your lifelines from birth until your current age. Make sure you label the high and low points in your life so that you can share your lifeline with the rest of us.

For Junior High Students

To help your students see how a lifeline looks, draw one before the lesson that depicts your own life. Take a minute or so to explain the high points and low points on your lifeline.

Make sure everyone understands the instructions, and then give students about five minutes to complete their lifelines. Walk around and help students who have trouble thinking back over their lives. Assure students that they'll not be *required* to share their lifelines with anyone else.

For Junior High Students

If a student is struggling to think of the high and low points of his or her life, ask questions such as these:
- **Did you really enjoy any vacations you took?**
- **What's the best class you've ever had?**
- **When did you meet your best friend?**
- **Was there someone close to you who died?**

When kids have finished, say: **Now let's go a little deeper. Look at all of the low points on your lifeline. These are probably the times when God seemed distant. The more you needed him, the harder he was to find. I want you to think about each of these low points and write down the results of that situation. Maybe you lost your best friend, but then you found a new friend who encouraged you in your faith.**

Give students time to think through the results of their struggles and write them down. Ask a few volunteers to share their lifelines with the rest of the group. Make sure they also share the *results* of the trials they went through and how God might have been working through those times.

Say: **Even though we don't always recognize it, when God seems most distant, he is usually most actively involved in our circumstances. Look at your lifeline again. Can you find a time God completely abandoned you?**

Read Isaiah 43:1-2 aloud, and then say: **God is always with you—even when it feels as if he's nowhere around. As your loving Father, God helped you survive and endure the difficult circumstances noted on your lifeline. You can put your trust in God because he is always with you.**

Living God's Truth

(10 minutes)

Say: **We can trust God to do what is best for us, but as we discovered in Matthew 7, he asks one thing of us. When we need something in life, God wants us to ask him. God already knows what we need, but he also values our relationship with him. God knows that we can't make it on our own and that we need to be totally dependent on him. Think back over the past month. What kinds of things have you asked God for?**

Give students a few minutes to write on the back of their lifelines the things they've been praying about lately.

Say: **Now I want you to think about the things you will be facing in the next few weeks that you'll need God to help you with. List those under your other requests.** After students have had a minute to add their requests, say: **Now review the needs you have listed. Are there any that are contrary to God's will for you? If so, cross them out. For example, if you prayed that God would not let you get caught taking money out of your mom's purse, God probably won't want to honor that request.**

After students have had a minute to cross out any requests that would not match with God's will, say: **I want you to take this list home and keep track of the ways God answers your requests. He may give you what you ask for, or he may decide it's not right for you at this time. In any case, try to see how God shows his faithfulness to you.**

Close in prayer, thanking God for being a perfect Father and committing to put your trust in him.

To Follow Up

> Create a bulletin board in your meeting place, and divide the board into two areas: "God's In-Box" and "God's Out-Box." Have small note-sized pieces of paper and thumbtacks nearby, and encourage students to write their prayer requests on slips of paper. Have teenagers tack the requests to "God's In-Box." Over the coming weeks, have kids keep track of God's responses to their prayer requests, and move the corresponding pieces of paper over to "God's Out-Box" once those prayers have been answered.

To Follow Up

> Take a video camera to a mall or shopping center, and have kids politely interview people by asking them to answer the question, "What worries you most in life?" Some people will be reticent to share, but many will be surprisingly straightforward and blunt. After the experience, watch the video with your students. Have teenagers explain how they feel about each worry.

To Follow Up

Challenge your students to consistently keep a prayer journal. At the beginning of every meeting, have kids list in their journals their requests and the ways God answers their prayers. Encourage kids to review the journals every few weeks to see God's faithfulness.

About God's Fatherhood

Imagine the best father you could ever ask for. Think of all of the best characteristics of your own father, and add to them the best qualities you've ever seen in other fathers. In Matthew 7:11, Jesus tells us that this ideal of fatherhood could never compare to our heavenly Father. Jesus shows us the true nature of our loving and tender eternal Father: He is not selfish, spiteful, or miserly with the gifts he gives. We don't have to beg and plead for gifts from our earthly fathers—why would we think God expects us to grovel for *his* help and approval? God knows exactly what we need, and he is delighted to give it to us when we ask.

For this reason, we have no cause to worry about our needs. As long as we seek God's kingdom first and look to him in times of need, God will fulfill every necessity of life.

Surviving Life

You win concert tickets in a radio contest. Go forward 1 space.	You break your leg while skiing. Go back 2 spaces.
Your dog dies. Go back 1 space.	You make the varsity volleyball team. Go forward 2 spaces.
You get accepted to Harvard University. Go forward 3 spaces.	You barely pass your math class. Stay put.
You fail your driving test twice. Go back 2 spaces.	Your parents get divorced. Go back 3 spaces.
You don't have any zits today. Stay put.	You are named Student of the Month. Go forward 2 spaces.
Your girlfriend or boyfriend breaks up with you. Go back 1 space.	You find an old penny in your drawer that's worth $100. Go forward 1 space.
You get along with your siblings. Go forward 1 space.	One of your parents loses his or her job. Go back 2 spaces.
You lose your friend's brand-new jacket. Go back 1 space.	You find the important homework you thought you threw away. Stay put.
You throw up in front of your whole English class. Go back 1 space.	Your friends from school want to visit your church. Go forward 2 spaces.
Your parents give you a new car for your birthday. Go forward 2 spaces.	Your pastor forgets your name. Go back 1 space.

Permission to photocopy this handout from *Understanding God Together* granted for local church use.
Copyright © Group Publishing, Inc., P.O. Box 481, Loveland, CO 80539.

Handout

My Lifeline

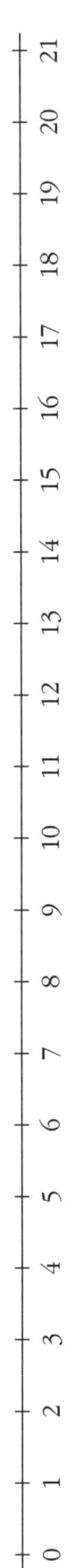

middle line

Permission to photocopy this handout from *Understanding God Together* granted for local church use.
Copyright © Group Publishing, Inc., P.O. Box 481, Loveland, CO 80539.

Because God is faithful,
you will never be alone.

Objectives

Through this lesson, students will
- reflect on times of loneliness,
- learn about God's faithfulness throughout the Bible,
- perform skits about God's faithfulness, and
- reflect on God's faithfulness in their lives.

For this lesson, you'll need

- Bibles
- paper
- pens
- copies of the "Story of Faithfulness: Then and Now" handout (p. 73)
- copies of the "Conclusion" handout (p. 74)

Understanding God's Faithfulness

Faithfulness is a commitment to be there for someone—especially in time of need, a commitment that may be increasingly difficult for today's teens to experience. In the face of the fragile relationships they may experience in their families, with friends, and in the world around them, kids need to know that God is faithful. Teenagers can always count on God to be there for them.

Throughout the Bible, God demonstrates his faithfulness by watching over his chosen people and providing his Son for all people. The past two thousand years of history continue to demonstrate how God is faithful in helping his church grow and influence the world.

Teenagers can also be encouraged by knowing that the faithfulness God has demonstrated to countless others throughout history is available to them as well. Teenagers can know that no matter how disappointing their earthly relationships may turn out to be, their relationship with God is secure.

Getting Started

(15 minutes)

If weather permits, do this activity outside. If not, choose an area where each student can be as secluded as possible. Lead kids to your chosen area, and give each teenager a sheet of paper and a pen.

Say: **I want each of you to find an area where you can be as secluded as possible. Once there, I want you to think about the time in your life when you felt most alone. Write down the circumstances and the feelings you dealt with. I'll tell you when it's time to stop. If you finish before I tell you to stop, sit quietly and reflect on your experience.**

Give kids five to eight minutes to write their experiences. Then call students together. Ask:

- **What emotions did you experience as you thought about your situation?**
- **What emotions did you experience when the event actually happened?**
- **Were there people who were involved in your experience? Explain.**
- **Why do you think it's so hard to be alone?**

Say: **We all face loneliness in our lives. Sometimes our loneliness comes from the breakdown of relationships. Sometimes it comes from difficult circumstances we have to endure. No matter what kind of loneliness we face, we can know that God is faithful and that we never have to be alone.**

God Is Faithful

(20 minutes)

Give each student a copy of the "Story of Faithfulness: Then and Now" handout (p. 73). Have students form pairs or trios, and assign a "chapter" of the handout to each student. Say: **The Bible is a long story of God's faithfulness. Read the introduction on your handout, and then study your assigned chapter. Read the Bible passage under your chapter heading, and write the answers to the questions. You'll have several minutes to explore your chapter.**

Give kids eight minutes to study their chapters.

> **For the Study**
>
> If you have time, have each student or group go through all the chapters and give each person or group a chance to summarize each section.

Say: **The Bible is a story of God's faithfulness. Each of you has looked at a brief part of that story. Now we'll hear a summary of some important parts of the story.**

Have the kids who studied chapter 1 summarize their Bible passages first, the students who worked on chapter 2 summarize their passages second, and so on. When all four Bible passages have been summarized, ask:

- **How were the people's situations in each chapter similar? different?**

- **Do you think the people felt alone in their situations? Explain.**
- **How did God's faithfulness show through in these situations?**
- **How do you think these situations changed the way the people felt about God?**
- **What are some other biblical examples of God's faithfulness?**

Say: **In the Bible, we see God's faithfulness again and again. God didn't leave his people when they needed him. In the same way, God will never leave you alone. Let me show you what I mean.**

What That Means for You
(15 minutes)

Have kids form groups of two to four. Give each group a copy of the "The Conclusion" handout (p. 74). Have each group follow the directions on its handout to prepare a skit for the class.

For High School Students

It may be helpful to include at least one high school student in each drama group to provide guidance in preparing the drama.

Give groups about five minutes to prepare their dramas. Then have groups perform their dramas for the rest of the students. After groups have finished their skits, ask:
- **What emotions did you experience while performing your skit?**
- **How did it feel to be alone or let down by others in the situation you dramatized?**
- **How did God's faithfulness help you in that situation?**
- **How can past examples of God's faithfulness help you when you have needs in the future?**

Say: **You will never be alone. God has demonstrated that truth in the lives of the people in the Bible and in our lives. Let's take a minute to thank God for his faithfulness.**

Gather kids in a circle, and have each student complete the following sentence prayer: "Father, thank you for showing me your faithfulness by…"

Living God's Truth
(10 minutes)

Lead kids back to the area you used in the "Getting Started" activity. Say: **We have seen that God's faithfulness means you will never be alone or apart from God. But sometimes it is hard to be alone *with* God.**

Have kids find a quiet place as they did earlier and spend time thinking about God's faithfulness to them. From this, students could read Bible passages, thank God in prayer, or simply meditate in silence. Join kids in the activity, and let the time for this activity end without adding any closing statements.

God is faithful 69

To Follow Up

Arrange an interview with someone who has historical knowledge of your church's or denomination's history. Kids could see how God's faithfulness blessed the lives of key people involved in your church's history.

To Follow Up

Create a history of your youth group. Interview other church members who know about the youth group. Get addresses or e-mail addresses of college students and young adults who could tell about their experiences with the group. Prepare a presentation for the church, and share it during a church potluck or another all-church gathering.

To Follow Up

Develop a "Never a Lonely Hearts Club" for your group. Decorate a shoe box with the club title. Have students write their names on pieces of paper and put the papers in the box when they're lonely. Each week, have kids each select a name from the box and call the person whose name they've selected. Remind kids to keep the names confidential.

To Follow Up

Have kids create a spiritual journal. Explain how this journal is like a spiritual diary. Kids often start a daily journal with enthusiasm and commitment, but if they miss a few days, become discouraged and quit. To avoid this, have kids commit to making a minimum of three entries a week rather than daily entries. Encourage kids to be completely open and honest with God in their journals.

Bible Insight

The verses immediately preceding 2 Timothy 4:16-18 explain the context of Paul's report of having been deserted. Paul personally indicted Alexander, a metalworker, for the "great deal of harm" he inflicted on Paul and for how he "strongly opposed" the gospel message. Perhaps Alexander had been responsible for Paul's arrest and imprisonment.

Although Paul lacked human support, he boldly proclaimed, "But the Lord stood at my side and gave me strength" (verse 17). Paul was able to proclaim the gospel in Caesar's court—spreading the message throughout Rome.

Paul closed this passage expressing confidence that God would protect him from attacks and bring him "safely to his heavenly kingdom." Although "kingdom of heaven" is used often in Matthew to mean God's reign, Paul was probably referring to the eternal realm of heaven. Knowing this, Paul exclaimed praise to the Lord in one of his many doxologies: "To him be glory for ever and ever. Amen."

About God's Faithfulness

While God's faithfulness is the same in the Old and New Testaments, it is demonstrated in different ways. Many of the promises made in the Old Testament have been fulfilled, and God's actions demonstrate a certainty that the others will be fulfilled in due time. In the New Testament, God's faithfulness is seen primarily in the redemption of Christ's ministry. Christ's life, ministry, death and resurrection, and the gift of the Holy Spirit all show the decisiveness of God's faithfulness in the redemption of the world.

A Story of Faithfulness: Then and Now

Instructions: Read the Bible passages, and answer the questions.

Introduction

God made a covenant promise to Abraham. God promised Abraham that his descendants would become a great nation that would take the land of Canaan. God promised that he would be Abraham's God.

Chapter 1. Famine in Israel

After Joseph was sold into slavery by his brothers, God made Joseph a mighty ruler in Egypt. God had Joseph prepare Egypt for a famine by storing food during abundant years. The Israelites, including Joseph's brothers and his father, were suffering because of the famine.

Read Genesis 42:1-5; 46:2-7.

- What would you have thought about God's faithfulness during the famine?
- How would your thoughts have changed after moving to Egypt?

Chapter 2. Exodus from Egypt

Moses was raised by his mother in the Egyptian Pharaoh's house. When Moses was grown, God explained that he would rescue the Israelite people by sending ten plagues against Egypt. After the tenth plague of death to the firstborn, Pharaoh released the Israelites. Pharaoh's army then chased the Israelites to the edge of the Red Sea.

Read Exodus 14:10-14, 21-23, 27-31.

- How would you have felt about God's faithfulness as Pharaoh's armies were approaching?
- How would you have felt after seeing Pharaoh's army drown in the sea?

Chapter 3. Return to Jerusalem

God blessed the Israelites, and they became a mighty nation. God sent prophets, judges, and kings to lead them. When the Israelites disobeyed God, he allowed them to be captured by foreign nations. But God promised some would return to rebuild his kingdom. Nehemiah was one of those chosen to return and rebuild the wall around the city of Jerusalem.

Read Nehemiah 2:1-6; 6:15-16; 8:9-12.

- What would you have thought about God's faithfulness when your city wall was torn down?
- How would you have felt after the wall was rebuilt and you heard God's commands for the first time?

Chapter 4. The Savior Comes

God sent his Son, born to a virgin girl. Jesus grew up and began his ministry. Jesus promised his kingdom would never end. The claim angered the Jewish leaders, and they convinced the Roman government to crucify Jesus as a criminal.

Read Luke 24:13-34.

- How would you have felt about God's faithfulness before you recognized Jesus?
- How would you have reacted when Jesus revealed himself?

The Conclusion

The Bible is a story of God's faithfulness from the beginning to the end of time. God has proven his faithfulness to his people. And God will continue to prove his faithfulness to you.

Read 2 Timothy 4:16-18, and discuss the following questions in your pair or group:
- How was God faithful to Paul?
- If God was faithful to Paul, why did Paul still face troubles?
- How does God's faithfulness help us face troubles?

Think about an experience in your life that was similar to Paul's. In your pair or group, discuss an example of God's faithfulness to you in that situation. Choose one example, and prepare a skit demonstrating that situation. Use the following questions to help you prepare:
- Who was involved in the experience?
- Where did this experience take place?
- When did it happen?
- How did you need God's help?
- How did you see God's faithfulness in the situation?
- How did God's Word help you?
- How did other Christians help you?
- How could the message of 2 Timothy 4:16-18 have helped your situation?

Because God is generous,
God has given you gifts to give.

Objectives

Through this lesson, students will
- use items to help others,
- learn from Scripture about God's gifts to his people,
- learn how historical figures helped others with the gifts God gave them, and
- evaluate how God has been generous to them.

For this lesson, you'll need

- Bibles
- a large trash bag of miscellaneous items as described on page 76
- tape
- small gift bags or paper sacks
- gift tags
- a marker
- paper
- newsprint
- copies of the "Discovering Spiritual Gifts" handout (pp. 83-84)
- pens

Understanding God's Generosity

"Riches are the least worthy gifts which God can give man. What are they to God's word, to bodily gifts, such as beauty and health, or to the gifts of the mind, such as understanding, skill, wisdom! Yet men toil for them day and night, and take no rest. Therefore God commonly gives riches to foolish people, to whom he gives nothing else" (Martin Luther, quoted in *12,000 Religious Quotations*, edited by Frank S. Mead).

" 'Twant me, 'twas the Lord. I always told him, 'I trust to you. I don't know where to go or what to do, but I expect you to lead me,' and he always did" (Harriet Tubman, quoted in *Familiar Quotations*, edited by John Bartlett).

"Our intellect and other gifts have been given to be used for God's greater glory, but sometimes they become the very god for us. That is the saddest part: we are losing our balance when this happens. We must free ourselves to be filled by God. Even God cannot fill what is full" (Mother Teresa, quoted in *The Book of Wisdom*).

Martin Luther championed God's Word and endeavored to share it with others. Harriet Tubman repeatedly risked her life by leading dozens of slaves to freedom. Mother Teresa devoted her life to helping the most destitute people in the world.

These people changed the world. But was it really them—or was it God working through them? God gives generously to his people in order to accomplish some great things in the world. He gave to Martin Luther, Harriet Tubman, and Mother Teresa, and he gives to your kids, too.

God can work through you and me. That is the ultimate in generosity! Your kids don't have to risk their lives or give up everything to use what God has given them. They just need to recognize that God has a plan and part of that plan is to liberally give us gifts to get his work done. The plan simply requires teenagers to responsibly use God's gifts.

Your kids shouldn't feel useless, hopeless, or abandoned by God; they can know that they are part of the solution. God has given each of them gifts that they can use to give to others.

Getting Started

(15 minutes)

Before class, you'll need to collect at least one item for each person and put the items in a large trash bag. You might collect items such as a water bottle, a scarf, sunglasses, a Bible, string, a flashlight, a hat, a ball, a bag of candy, a party favor, and a kazoo. To help kids get the most out of the activity, mix obviously useful items with odd ones and choose items that kids can use immediately.

When kids arrive, have them form pairs. You can pair up with a student yourself if you have an uneven number of kids. Have each person take a turn selecting an item from the trash bag without looking. Say: **In your pairs, you'll need to figure out a way to use your item to do something helpful or encouraging for your partner. For example, you could play a tune with a kazoo to make your partner laugh, or you could use a water bottle to give your partner a drink.** Give kids about five minutes to find helpful ways to use their items. Then gather students together, and ask:

- **Was this activity easy or difficult? awkward or natural? Explain.**
- **How did you figure out how to use your item?**
- **How did it feel to use your item to help someone?**
- **Do you have gifts you can use to help others? Explain.**
- **What happens to the gifts God gives you if you don't use them?**
- **How does it make you feel to know that you have gifts to give?**

Say: **Just as we can use tools to help others, God has given us gifts to use to help others, too. We can use them individually or collectively to show God's generosity to others. Sometimes it's easy to focus on what we don't have. But using what God has given us to give to others can show us that God is generous and has given us many gifts. Now let's learn what kinds of gifts God has given his people.**

God Is Generous

(15 minutes)

Before class, write the following Scripture references on separate strips of paper: Genesis 1:29-30; Numbers 6:24-26; Psalm 115:16; John 3:16; Acts 2:38; Romans 6:23; Romans 12:6-8; and 1 Corinthians 12:7-11. Make one strip for each student; it's OK to use one Scripture more than once. If you have fewer than eight students, you can put two or more Scriptures on one strip of paper. Place each strip in a gift bag, and seal the bag with tape. Write each student's name on a gift tag, and attach the tags to the gift bags. Make sure you prepare extra bags for visitors.

Say: **Look at all these gifts! Looks like everyone here gets one!** Distribute the gifts and Bibles.

Have kids each find a partner, open their gifts, and read their Scriptures to their partners. Give kids about five minutes to tell each other about the gifts the Scriptures reflect and how they've enjoyed or recognized the gifts in their own lives. For example, students with the Acts 2:38 "gift" could say, "I've recognized God's gift of the Holy Spirit in my life when he helps me understand a difficult passage in Scripture." Then have pairs discuss these questions:

● **How has God been generous to you—either through gifts he's given you or through what others have done for you?**

● **Why do you think God gives people gifts?**

Say: **When we think about God's generosity, we typically think about what God has done *for* us. But it's important to realize that God is incredibly generous through what he *gives* us. Unlike most gifts, God's gifts are meant to be shared with and given to others. Let me show you what I mean.**

What That Means for You

(25 minutes)

Have a volunteer read aloud 1 Corinthians 12:1-11. Ask:

● **What does this passage tell you about the gifts God gives?**
● **What does it tell you about why God gives gifts?**
● **How are these gifts different? the same?**
● **What are we supposed to do with these gifts?**

For Junior High Students

You may want to explain the cultural background of verses 1-3. Many new Christians in Corinth had converted from pagan religions. Because of the common practice of divination and "prophecy" in pagan religions, the church in Corinth needed direction about how to determine right prophecy from wrong prophecy. Therefore Paul explained the "litmus test" in verse 3—that no one could say, "Jesus is Lord" except by the Holy Spirit.

Help your kids understand the meaning of verse 3 in their own lives—that when they say and believe that "Jesus is Lord," they also have evidence of the Holy Spirit working through them.

For Junior High Kids

In verses 4-6, Paul emphasizes the unity of all the gifts. Help your younger students understand that no matter what gifts we use, it's important to remember that they come from the same Spirit. It's also good to remember that they're all of equal importance. "Paul emphasizes that all the gifts are different but all are useful; hence a Christian with one gift is not more or less important than another Christian with a different gift" (Craig S. Keener, *The IVP Bible Background Commentary: New Testament*).

Tape a sheet of newsprint to a wall, and draw a line down the middle of the newsprint. In the first column, write, "What did God give? Why?" In the second column, write, "What happened as a result?" Then tell kids to think about the questions on the newsprint as they listen to stories about historical Christians.

Read aloud Acts 8:26-40, and then have kids discuss the questions written on the newsprint. As kids are discussing the two questions, write their responses on the newsprint.

Read aloud: **Martin Luther's father wanted him to be a lawyer, but he knew God had called him to be a monk. He struggled in his faith until he found security not in depending on himself or others, but in trusting God completely.**

Luther built a successful monastic and academic career, but his soul was troubled. At age thirty, after intensely reading Psalms, Galatians, and Romans, he dedicated his life to teaching God's Word as the ultimate authority. Concerned about the biblical illiteracy of the lower classes, he translated the Bible directly from the Greek and Hebrew texts into German. He then made worship services more "user friendly" by performing the traditional Latin mass in German. Also seeing a need to educate people at an early age, he began a campaign for Christian schools and worked with parents and pastors to provide proper education for children.

Luther was also a prolific writer. He wrote psalms and sermons and was a gifted linguist, theologian, and translator. He wrote many volumes on a variety of topics. Some of his works include *The Freedom of a Christian Man, Lectures on Galatians,* and the song "A Mighty Fortress." All of Luther's works were dedicated to reforming the way people saw the role of the church and the role of the Scriptures.

In 1517 he wrote his most famous work, *95 Theses,* which mapped out what he saw as misguided teachings in the church. Although his opinions conflicted with other church authorities, Luther's lifelong aim was to bring peace and reconciliation to the church and to teach constantly the power of God's Word above all.

Martin Luther once said to his mother, "Be of good cheer and thank [God] joyfully for such great grace! For He who has begun [His work] in you will also graciously complete it, since we are unable to help ourselves in such matters." (Sources: J.D. Douglas and Philip W. Comfort, eds., *Who's Who in Christian History;* and Stephen Rost, ed., *Martin Luther*).

Again, have the kids discuss the two questions you wrote on the newsprint; then write their responses on the newsprint.

Then read aloud: **Harriet Tubman was a slave in Maryland in the late 1800s. When she discovered that she was going to be sold, she escaped, making the dangerous trip to Philadelphia, where she eventually found work.**

Not content to save just herself from slavery, Harriet made at least nineteen trips back to Maryland, leading dozens of slaves to freedom. Each time she returned to the North, she found a new job to fund the next trip.

Harriet Tubman was called "Moses" by the slaves whom she led to freedom. A deeply religious person, Harriet said she was acting on a divine command to free her people.

Colonel Thomas Wentworth Higginson said about Harriet Tubman, "We have had the greatest heroine of the age here, Harriet Tubman, a black woman, and a fugitive slave, who has been back eight times secretly and brought out in all sixty slaves with her...Her talks of adventure are beyond anything in fiction and her ingenuity and generalship are extraordinary... She is jet black and cannot read or write, only talk, besides acting" (Colonel Thomas Wentworth Higginson, quoted in *The Book of Wisdom*).

As kids again discuss the two questions, write their responses on the newsprint.

Then read aloud: **At age eighteen, Mother Teresa left her home country of Yugoslavia and began her missionary work. She moved to Calcutta, India, and taught geography at St. Mary's High School.**

After seventeen years, Mother Teresa became disconcerted by the contrast between her comfortable life in the convent and the life of the poor she served. She asked to be released from the convent to live among and help the poor, the lepers, abandoned children, and the dying. For more than four decades, Mother Teresa worked in the slums of Calcutta, India—one of the most destitute areas in the world.

In an interview with Time magazine, Mother Teresa was asked if she possessed any extraordinary spiritual qualities that allowed her to work with societal outcasts. She replied, "I don't think so. I don't claim anything of the work. It is [God's] work. I am like a little pencil in his hand. That's all. He does the thinking. He does the writing. The pencil has nothing to do with it. The pencil has only to be allowed to be used" (C. Douglas Weaver, ed., *From Our Christian Heritage*).

As kids discuss the two questions on the newsprint, write their responses in the appropriate columns. Then ask:

- Do you think God uses us to share his generosity? Why or why not?
- How do these stories reflect how God uses us to share his generosity?
- What have these stories taught you about the gifts God gives us?
- What do you think about the importance of using the gifts God gives us?
- Do you think these people possessed extraordinary qualities? Why or why not?
- After hearing these stories, do you think God has given you gifts to give? Why or why not?

Say: **Martin Luther, Harriet Tubman, and Mother Teresa were all just ordinary people like you and me. But as 1 Corinthians teaches, if we believe that Jesus is Lord, we are equally important tools in God's hands. And just as Martin Luther, Harriet Tubman, and Mother Teresa discovered and used the gifts God gave them, you can discover and use the gifts God has given you.**

For Junior High Students

If students have a hard time thinking of gifts God has given them, mention to them that the Bible cites gifts such as encouragement, wisdom, and teaching.

Living God's Truth

(15 minutes)

Have kids return to their pairs. Ask:
- **What gifts do you think God has given you?**
- **What gifts do you think your partner has used?**

Hand each person a pen and a copy of the "Discovering Spiritual Gifts" handout (p. 83). Tell kids to find an area of the room to be by themselves. Say: **God is going to give you gifts to use throughout your life, and you'll need to experiment with different gifts in order to find what your true gifts are. Some initial self-evaluation can boost your confidence and get you started, so take a few minutes to answer the questions on your handout. First pray that God will help you discover and use the gifts he gives you.**

After five minutes, gather kids back together. Ask:
- **Was it easy or difficult to evaluate yourself? Explain.**
- **Do you think it's more important to figure out what your gifts are or to share your gifts with others? Explain.**

Say: **Because God is generous, he has given you gifts to give. While it's comforting to evaluate your gifts, the important thing is to use them to help others.**

Tape a sheet of newsprint to a wall, and write the different gifts from the handout across the top of the newsprint. Have kids call out ways to use each gift. For example, for the gift of encouragement, someone might say, "Hug a friend." Encourage kids to be creative and think of lots of ideas for each gift.

Then have kids form pairs. With their partners, have kids choose one gift from their handouts that they'd like to try to use during the week. Have kids circle the gift they'd like to use and write several ideas from the newsprint that lists how to use the gifts. Encourage partners to follow up with each other during the week to ensure everyone tries to use a gift.

To Follow Up

Have your kids plan an all-day service project for the church. Your project might be planting a garden on the church grounds or cleaning the sanctuary. Allow kids to discover their spiritual gifts by letting them serve on different committees. For example, if you decide to plant a garden, one student might organize a group of planters to explore the gift of service, and after the garden is planted, another student might plan an outdoor Bible study on Creation to explore the gift of teaching. If you have time, get your kids to rotate their participation on the committees to allow them to explore more than one spiritual gift. Here are some other service-project ideas you can do for the church:
- volunteer to help run the VBS program,
- take on a painting or remodeling project,
- lead a session of Sunday school for one of the elementary grade levels,
- plan a picnic to honor the church's volunteers, or
- help decorate the church for Easter or Christmas.

Encourage students to work on the aspects of the service project that they feel comfortable with as well as aspects they've never tried to work on before.

To Follow Up

Have your kids use their "Discovering Spiritual Gifts" handout to interview their families and friends. Students can alter the questions they ask their families and friends to answer about themselves while they use a video camera or a tape recorder to record the sessions. At a later session, review the interviews with your students; at the end of the interviews, record your students' reactions to the interviews. Also be sure to record your students' commitments to exploring or practicing their spiritual gifts.

To Follow Up

Work with your clergy to plan a worship service on spiritual gifts for the congregation. Include a reading of the different Scriptures that mention spiritual gifts. You might also include a segment in which students talk about times they've witnessed others' spiritual gifts in action. Be sure your entire class participates in some way, and remind kids that if they are unsure about their spiritual gifts, this is a good time to explore them.

About God's Generosity

The greatest gift to the world was Jesus. But when Jesus ascended into heaven, God didn't abandon his people. Part of God's plan was to give even more to his people. In John 14:25-27, Christ told the disciples that although he would be physically leaving, the Holy Spirit would come to teach them "all things" and remind them of what Jesus taught.

So on the day of Pentecost, recorded in Acts 2, the Holy Spirit came upon the church. God gave his people the gift of the Spirit for two reasons, according to Charles Stanley: to give every believer a "significant role in the body of Christ" and to ensure "that believers work together to accomplish His overall purpose." The entire book of Acts stands as a compelling record of what God can accomplish through the Holy Spirit. The Christian church was born and flourished—even as its leaders were persecuted.

In 1 Corinthians, Romans, Ephesians, and 1 Peter, each discussion of spiritual gifts or roles in the church emphasizes that our gifts are used to edify the Body of Christ. God didn't give us the Holy Spirit to make us feel proud. "His plan to meet the needs of His people is *His people.* That is why He has gifted us."

"Our gifts allow us to become channels through which the very life and ministry of Christ flow. When we exercise our gifts for the common good, we manifest the person of Christ on the earth." This way, we can be involved in accomplishing God's plan.

(Quoted from Charles Stanley, "You Gotta Have Parts," Discipleship Journal, issue ninety, 1995).

Discovering Spiritual Gifts

Read about each of the following spiritual gifts, and write your answers to the questions that follow.

Encouragement—The Spirit-given ability to support others, giving them courage and hope.
- Do you like to help people who are weary or frustrated to feel better? Write about a time you've helped someone in this way.

- Do people like to talk to you about their problems? Explain.

- How do you think you could use the gift of encouragement to help others?

Evangelism—The Spirit-given ability to tell others about Jesus Christ and help them know Jesus personally.
- Do you feel a strong need to tell others about Jesus Christ? Write about a time you've told someone about Jesus.

- Do you like to invite people to church activities? Explain.

- How do you think you could use the gift of evangelism to help others?

Faith—The Spirit-given ability to unquestioningly believe in God while being assured that God always does what is best.
- Do you usually feel confident that God can take care of any situation, no matter how bad things get? Explain.

- Do you usually feel positive that God can help you through good times and bad times? Explain.

- How do you think you could use the gift of faith to help others?

Giving—The Spirit-given ability to give time, energy, and money where it's needed.
- Do you give freely to others because you know that God will meet your needs? Write about a time you gave to others.

Permission to photocopy this handout from *Understanding God Together* granted for local church use.
Copyright © Group Publishing, Inc., P.O. Box 481, Loveland, CO 80539.

- Do you really enjoy giving time and money to others? Explain.

- How do you think you could use the gift of giving to help others?

Leadership—The Spirit-given ability to motivate others to do work for the Lord.
- When you're with a group of people, do you like to take charge? Explain.

- Do your friends look to you to make decisions for the group? Write about a time you led others.

- How do you think you could use the gift of leadership to help others?

Mercy—The Spirit-given ability to comfort people without judging them.
- When you see disadvantaged people, do you feel very sympathetic? Explain.

- Do you feel patient with people who have problems and try to help them? Write about a time you had enough patience to help someone.

- How do you think you could use the gift of mercy to help others?

Service—The Spirit-given ability to assist and serve others.
- Do you enjoy helping others with work even if you won't get any credit? Write about a time you unselfishly helped someone.

- Do your friends tell you that you're helpful? Explain.

- How do you think you could use the gift of service to help others?

Teaching—The Spirit-given ability to clearly and accurately relate God's Word and truth.
- Do you make a point to study the Bible regularly? Explain.

- Do you really enjoy sharing what you learn with others? Write about a time you've taught others.

- How do you think you could use the gift of teaching to help others?

Because God is merciful,
you can look to God for help.

Objectives

Through this lesson, students will
- learn about God's mercy toward our repeated mistakes,
- compare our society's mercy with God's,
- create a personal reminder of God's mercy, and
- seek God's mercy.

For this lesson, you'll need

- Bibles
- newsprint
- tape
- a marker
- a knife
- self-hardening clay (from a craft store)
- carving tools such as toothpicks, craft knives, or pencils
- paper towels

Understanding God's Mercy

It seems simple: Our loving God wants a relationship with us. But through sin, we keep rejecting him. Even though we've done nothing to deserve a relationship with God, he knows we need it and God desires it. So God shows us mercy, forgiving us again and again. God may not remove the natural consequences of our sin, but he still loves us and provides a way for relationship with him. His mercy is endless.

Although the message of mercy seems simple, it may be a difficult concept for your teenagers to grasp. When someone hurts them, they may react harshly. When they see others making mistakes, they may feel judgmental rather than merciful. Teenagers may think God rejects them when they sin. They don't realize that God is with them before they sin and during their sin, wanting them to turn to him for strength, wisdom, and forgiveness. Your kids need to understand that it's precisely when they mess up that they need God the most. God won't reject them; mercifully, he'll keep loving them and healing them.

Getting Started

(10 minutes)

In this activity, kids will call out words of a Bible verse while you try to write the verse on newsprint. While you write, you'll intentionally make repeated mistakes.

Tape a sheet of newsprint to a wall. As kids arrive, have them gather on the floor around the newsprint. Have kids open their Bibles to Deuteronomy 4:31a: "For the Lord your God is a merciful God; he will not abandon or destroy you."

Say: **I'd like to write that verse on this sheet of newsprint; please read it to me so I can get it right.**

As kids call out words, make repeated mistakes. For example, if someone calls out, "God is a merciful God," you could write, "Is God a merciful God?" or "Merciful is a God." Sprinkle in questions such as "I'm sorry—could you say that again?" and "Is this right?"

Keep making mistakes for a minute or two, scribbling out words and lines and starting over again and again. After you finally get it right, ask:

- **What was your reaction to my repeated mistakes?**
- **How were my repeated mistakes like sin? different?**
- **How was my asking you for help similar to asking God for help when we sin? different?**
- **How was your repeated effort to help me write the verse correctly similar to God's mercy? different?**
- **How do you think God reacts to our repeated mistakes and sins? Explain.**

Say: **It seems that no matter how hard we try, we all continue to make mistakes. The good news is that God is merciful, so we can always turn to him when we sin. Just as I kept asking you for help while writing the Bible verse, we can keep looking to God for help when we sin.**

To better understand the depth of God's mercy, let's compare the way our society deals with wrongdoings with the way God might deal with them.

God Is Merciful

(20 minutes)

Tape another sheet of newsprint to a wall. Say: **Theodore Kaczynski mailed packages containing explosives to sixteen people throughout the United States. With his "mail bombs," he killed three people and injured twenty-nine over a period of seventeen years** ("Calif. Won't Prosecute Kaczynski," from the Internet, Associated Press, www.wire.ap.org). Ask:

- **If you had been on the jury during Kaczynski's trial, what would you have sentenced him to?**

As kids call out possibilities, write their ideas on newsprint. Then have the kids vote on the appropriate sentence.

Then say: **Robert Riggio approached priests across the United States, posing as a parishioner who was down on his luck. He conned fifty priests out of a collective $130,000 with his tales of woe** (Selwyn Raab, "Man Accused of Duping Pastor of $1.4 Million," from the Internet, New York Times, www.nytimes.com). Ask:

- **If you had been on the jury, what would you have sentenced Robert Riggio to?**

As kids call out possibilities, write their ideas on newsprint. Then have the kids vote for one sentence.

Say: **Fife Symington, a former Arizona governor, was convicted of cheating lenders in a real estate scheme. When he wanted people to lend him money to buy a piece of property, he gave them false financial statements to convince them that the property would be profitable.** Ask:

- **If you had been on the jury, what would you have sentenced Fife Symington to?**

Write down kids' ideas, and have them vote for one sentence.

Say: **Now here are the actual sentences: Theodore Kaczynski pleaded guilty and was sentenced to life in prison; Robert Riggio was sentenced to two years in prison; and Fife Symington was sentenced to two and a half years in prison, a $60,000 fine, and five years' probation.** Ask:

- **How were the sentences you came up with different from the actual sentences?**
- **Why do you think your sentences were different?**
- **What do you think God thinks about the crimes these people committed? the punishments?**
- **How do you think God's reaction to those crimes would differ from society's reaction?**

Say: **In our society, people who commit crimes are punished. And that's not always a bad way to handle things. God is perfectly just and fair, which tells us we should be responsible for our sins. God doesn't necessarily rescue us from the natural consequences of all our sins. But God's justice includes another aspect—his mercy.**

Have kids read Micah 7:18-19. Say: **To understand Micah's words, you may need some background. For thousands of years, God had been trying to set the people of Israel on the right track. God corrected, disciplined, and punished the Israelites, but they continued to follow other gods and leaders. Time after time, they defied God. But God kept pursuing them.** Ask:

- **Why do you think God continued to watch over Israel?**
- **How did God show mercy to Israel?**
- **What does Micah mean when he says that God doesn't "stay angry forever but delight[s] to show mercy"?**
- **Based on this Scripture, what do you think mercy is?**
- **What would it take for you to feel mercy toward the criminals we talked about?**
- **If you had mercy on these people, how would you act toward them?**
- **How do you think God acts toward and feels about the criminals?**
- **How do you think God's mercy affects your life?**

Have kids read Micah 5:1-5. Say: **This prophecy is about Jesus, whose life and death were God's ultimate act of mercy. In his life on earth, Jesus demonstrated true mercy as he listened, taught, and healed people. Then through Jesus' death on the cross, God made it possible for everyone to have a relationship with him despite our sin.** Ask:

● **How do you feel, knowing that Jesus' death demonstrates God's mercy?**

Say: **Throughout history, God has been merciful toward his people. So when we sin, instead of running away from God out of shame, we need to know that we can look to God for help. Let's think about what that means.**

What That Means for You
(15 minutes)

Use a knife to cut two small pieces of self-hardening clay for each student. Set out paper towels and carving tools such as toothpicks, carving knives, and pencils. Then say: **With one of your portions of clay, make a symbol that demonstrates what life would be like without God's mercy. Before you create your symbol, read Ephesians 2:1-5 for inspiration. When you've finished creating your symbol, read 1 John 1:8-9, and then create another symbol that demonstrates what God's mercy is like.**

When kids have finished, have each person share his or her symbols by asking each person these questions:

● **What do your symbols stand for?**

● **How have you seen God's mercy in your life?**

If you have access to an oven, follow the clay's package directions to harden the clay. Otherwise, make sure kids know the directions so they can harden the clay at home.

Encourage kids to take their symbols home and place them where they will see them throughout the day as reminders that we can turn to our merciful God for help.

Ask:

● **What would it take to make God so angry that he wouldn't want anything more to do with you? Explain.**

● **How do you feel about God when you've done something wrong? Why?**

● **When is the easiest time to turn to God for help? the hardest?**

Say: **Based on what we've learned about God's mercy, we know that it extends to each and every one of us. But sometimes we're not prepared to turn to God when we need him most. So let's think about what we can do to make sure we turn to God.**

Living God's Truth

(10 minutes)

Read aloud 1 John 1:9.

Ask:
- **If God knows what our sins are, why do we have to confess them?**
- **What does confessing do?**
- **Is God merciful to those who don't confess their sins? Why or why not?**
- **Is God merciful to you if you forget to confess a sin? Explain.**
- **According to this Scripture, is God ever unmerciful to those who confess their sins? Why or why not?**
- **How can the suggestions in this Scripture help you before you sin? after you sin?**

Say: **Turn to someone and tell him or her of a time that God forgave you or someone you know.** Give students a minute to share. Have kids spread out as much as the room allows.

Say: **We're going to take some time to seek God's mercy. God is ready to help those who turn to him, so don't be afraid to confess your sin to God. Ask God to bring sins to your mind that you need to confess to him. Wait for a few minutes as God directs you. When God brings something to mind, simply tell him that you're sorry and that you need his forgiveness. Then ask God to help you avoid committing the sin again.**

Give kids about five minutes to go through the process of repentance. After five minutes, pray aloud: **God, thank you for completely forgiving all of the sins we confessed today. Thank you for your mercy and for helping us. In Jesus' name, amen.**

To Follow Up

Hold a candlelight vigil to teach your teenagers that they need to show mercy to others as God has shown mercy to them. At the vigil, ask kids to talk about people who have hurt them and then light candles for those people. Pray that kids will be able to forgive those who hurt them, and then encourage kids to pray for those people.

To Follow Up

To extend God's mercy to others, have your teenagers participate in ministry to inmates. Teenagers can either write to prison inmates (you may want to get parental permission for this), or they can send care packages to the children of prison inmates. Contact Prison Fellowship Ministries at
- Box 17500, Washington D.C. 20041
- phone: (703) 478-0100
- Web site: www.pfm.org

Specify "Prison Fellowship Family Ministry Program" if you're interested in sending care packages.

To Follow Up

Ask your teenagers to read newspapers during the week. Have them look for and cut out stories of people they think may need to accept God's mercy. Kids could collect the stories in a folder and pray every day that God will show his mercy to those people and that they'll accept it.

Bible Insight

How could Micah be so sure of God's mercy and forgiveness? After all, Israel had been perpetually disobeying God. "Micah…prophesied during the eighth century B.C., a time when Israel and Judah had risen to heights of economic affluence but had fallen to depths of spiritual decadence" (*The Expositor's Bible Commentary*). Not only were Israelites practicing pagan religions, but they were also cheating their own poor. Micah knew that God would judge Israel accordingly, but he also knew God balances justice with mercy.

Micah had hope. After all, God's covenant with Abraham and Jacob was to last forever. Despite Israel's sinfulness, Micah was confident in God's mercy. He knew that God wouldn't turn his back on Israel forever. And he was right. As he prophesied in Micah 5:1-4, a new "ruler" would restore the glory of Israel. That ruler was Jesus, who made it possible for *everyone* to have a relationship with God.

About God's Mercy

In Romans 9, Paul discusses how God elects his people. God's election is not based on our desires or efforts, but on God's mercy. "God has mercy on whom he wants to have mercy, and he hardens whom he wants to harden" (Romans 9:18).

The idea of election leaves room for speculation: How and why does God choose certain people to receive his mercy? Some believe that God knows beforehand who will accept Christ. Others say God chooses who will accept Christ and rejects the others for reasons we do not understand. Some suggest God's election is for Jesus as his Son, and those with faith will share in a corporate election.

As the Zondervan Pictorial Encyclopedia of the Bible explains, part of the mystery of God's mercy is that its meaning (and translation) is many faceted: "Basic to the concept is God's care for man in his wretchedness and creatureliness. This emotionally based response manifests itself in His redemptive acts. The man responding to God sees in himself one who has received mercy; therefore he in turn must show mercy to his fellow man."

How or why God chooses his people may not be clear, but Paul says "Why?" is not the question we should ask: "Shall what is formed say to him who formed it, 'Why did you make me like this?' Does not the potter have the right to make out of the same lump of clay some pottery for noble purposes and some for common use?" (Romans 9:20b-21).

God's mercy is evident. And it is clear that God's mercy is the gift given for those who believe. Paul explains how God gives us mercy even when we don't deserve it: "Like the rest, we were by nature objects of wrath. But because of his great love for us, God, who is rich in mercy, made us alive with Christ even when we were dead in transgressions" (Ephesians 2:3b-5a).

God *should* be angry with us when we sin. He has the power to strike us down or reject us when we go against his will. Instead, God uses his power to see those headed for destruction, to show them mercy, to lead them to repentance, and to lead them to his glory. And God showed us the ultimate act of mercy by giving his Son, Jesus Christ.

Because God is majestic,
God is worthy of our praise.

Objectives

Through this lesson, students will
- learn to see God's majesty all around them,
- explore the majesty and praise in Psalm 145,
- acknowledge the presence of God's majesty in their own lives, and
- see praise as the natural response to God's majesty.

For this lesson, you'll need

- Bibles
- a TV
- a VCR
- two videos as described on page 94
- aluminum foil
- markers
- scissors
- tape
- newsprint
- paper
- a three-hole paper punch
- a three-ring binder
- pens

Understanding God's Majesty

"O Lord, our Lord, how majestic is your name in all the earth" (Psalm 8:1).

"God is in all things and in every place. There is not a place in the world in which He is not most truly present" (Saint Francis of Sales, *Sermons*).

"There can be no doubt but that everything in the world, by the beauty of its order, and the evidence of a determinate and beneficial purpose which pervades it, testifies that some supreme efficient Power must have pre-existed, by which the whole was ordained for a specific end" (John Milton, *A Treatise on Christian Doctrine*).

Look around. Where do you see evidence of God's majesty? Psalmists, poets, and people of all ages have seen God's majesty all around them. In nature, in order, in power, and even in the tiniest details of life, they have found God's handiwork. Do you see it?

What about your students? Just like the psalmists and poets of the past, your students can learn to see God all around them. It's not merely a pretty sunset; it's a reflection in the sky of God's creativity. It's not merely a helping hand; it's an expression of God's love. Your kids simply need to learn to see God's signature in daily events.

As your kids learn to see God's majesty all around them, they'll grow closer to God and learn about him. They'll learn that God touches their lives in countless ways. They'll find God's majesty too wonderful to understand completely. But they'll see God's goodness, righteousness, power, love, and eternal nature, and they'll respond with praise. God's majesty can be overwhelming; it is so completely *majestic*. How can we respond but to praise him?

Getting Started
(15 minutes)

For this activity, you'll need to choose two short segments of movies or TV shows that reflect God's majesty in some way. One segment should clearly reflect God's majesty, and the other one should be a little less obvious.

For the first, more obvious segment, you could use a miracle scene from *Touched By an Angel,* a closing segment on nature from *CBS Sunday Morning,* a Mount Sinai scene from *The Ten Commandments,* or a portion of a TV sermon. For the second, less obvious segment, you could use a fly-fishing scene from *A River Runs Through It,* the opening scene of *The Lion King,* the moment in *How the Grinch Stole Christmas* when the Grinch's heart grows three sizes, or the closing scene of *It's a Wonderful Life.*

Before class be sure you cue the tapes to the segments you wish to show, and review the segments to be sure they are inoffensive and appropriate for your kids. After kids have arrived, ask:

● **How would you define majesty?**
● **What do you think of when I say, "God is majestic"?**

Gather kids around the TV, and say: **I'm going to show you a couple of video segments. As you watch, look for evidence of God's majesty.**

Show the video segment in which God's majesty is more obvious. Then ask:

● **What's your reaction to this video segment?**
● **Did you see evidence of God's majesty in this segment? Explain.**
● **If you've seen something like this before, did you notice God's majesty then? Why or why not?**

Then show the video segment in which God's majesty is less obvious. Afterward, ask:

● **What's your reaction to this video segment?**
● **Did you see evidence of God's majesty in this segment? Explain.**
● **Was it more difficult to detect God's majesty in this segment? Why or why not?**
● **If you've seen something like this before, did you notice God's majesty then? Why or why not?**

Read aloud the following quote:

"It is surprising how easy it is to hear music in the waves, and songs in the wild whisperings of the winds; to see God everywhere in the stones, in the rocks, in the rippling brooks, and hear him everywhere, in the lowing of cattle, in the rolling of thunder, and in the fury of tempests" (Charles Haddon Spurgeon, *Sermons*).

Ask:
- **What did you think about as I read this quote?**
- **What made the author aware of God's majesty?**
- **Have those things ever made you aware of God's majesty before? Explain.**

Read aloud the following quote:

Why does God bring thunderclouds and disasters when we want green pastures and still waters? Bit by bit we find, behind the clouds, the Father's feet; behind the lightning, an abiding day that has no night; behind the thunder, "a still small voice" that comforts with a comfort that is unspeakable (Oswald Chambers, *In the Presence of His Majesty*).

Ask:
- **What did you think about as I read this quote?**
- **What made this author aware of God's majesty?**
- **Has that ever made you aware of God's majesty before? Explain.**

Then read aloud the following quote:

"God's…power is not so much displayed in the vastness of the heavens, or the luster of the stars, or the orderly arrangement of the universe or his perpetual watching over it, as in his condescension to our weak nature. We marvel at the way the sublime entered a state of lowliness" (Saint Gregory of Nyssa, *Address on Religious Instruction*).

For Junior High Students

You may need to explain the meaning of the word "condescension" to some of your kids. Before you ask the discussion questions, explain that "condescension" is the act of doing something beneath one's dignity.

For Junior High Students

You may want to make the quotes available to your students by writing them on a sheet of newsprint and taping the sheet to a wall. Doing so will give kids a chance to process the quotes.

Ask:
- **How does the fact that God entered a state of lowliness demonstrate his majesty?**
- **What things in your life have made you aware of God's majesty?**
- **How do you think we should recognize God's majesty?**
- **Why is it important to recognize God's majesty?**

For Junior High Students

Younger students may not understand why we should recognize God's majesty. By recognizing God's majesty, we can continually appreciate what God has done for us. You may want to ask these additional questions to help kids who are struggling with the question:
- How does it make you feel to think about God's majesty?
- How can recognizing God's majesty help us see all God has done for us?

Say: **We can find God's majesty in many places—from a sunset to Christ's victory over death. Seeing God's majesty helps us to remember that God is worthy of our praise. Let's learn how we can recognize God's majesty in many places.**

God Is Majestic
(25 minutes)

If you have time, lead kids to a spot outdoors where they can see God's creation. Have kids discuss the majesty they see before them.

Set out aluminum foil, markers, scissors, and tape; then have kids form pairs. Have pairs discuss how everyday events and items can reflect God's majesty. Then tell pairs to find as many things in the room as possible that reflect God's majesty. When a pair finds something, partners can cut out a star from the aluminum foil, write on the star how that item reflects God's majesty, and then tape the star to the item. For example, someone might write on a star, "When people write hymns, they share God's majesty with others" and then tape that star to a hymnal.

Allow kids to work for about five minutes, and then have them walk around the room to see what others have tagged. After a couple of minutes, call kids back together. Ask:
- **What did you learn about God's majesty from this activity?**
- **How did you see God's majesty reflected around the room?**
- **What does the number of stars tell you about God's majesty?**
- **If we found this much majesty in one room, what does that tell you about God's majesty in the whole universe? in your life?**
- **What do you think your response should be to God's majesty?**

Distribute Bibles, and have several volunteers read aloud Psalm 145. Tape up a sheet of newsprint, and create two columns. Label one column "We know God is majestic because..." and the other column "We praise God by..."

Say: **Look at the psalm again. Then call out different responses to God's majesty that the psalmist cited. For example, you could look at verse 8 and say, "We know God is majestic because he is gracious and compassionate." Then call out different things the psalmist cited as responses to God's majesty. For example, you could look at verse 7 and say, "We praise God by singing joyfully."**

When kids have called out everything they can find for both columns, ask:
- What made the psalmist aware of God's majesty?
- Why do you think the psalmist wrote these words?
- How did the psalmist say we can praise God for his majesty?
- Why do you think it's important to praise God?
- What are some ways to praise God?

Say: **Recognizing God's majesty can help us see how much God has done for us. It also helps us learn who God is. And when we see who God really is, our natural response is to understand that God is worthy of our praise.**

What That Means for You

(15 minutes)

Have kids spread out so they're as secluded as possible. Say: **One reason we need to learn about God's majesty is to become aware of the many things God has done for us personally.**

At the beginning of class, you heard quotes from people whose lives had been touched by God's majesty in God's creation, in God's comfort, and in Christ's humanity. Then you read the words of a psalmist whose life had been touched in many different ways by God's majesty—through God's greatness, mighty acts, wonderful works, and everything else we wrote on the newsprint. Now I'd like you to think about your own life. Using what you've learned today about how we see God's majesty, think about how you have been affected *personally* by God's majesty. Maybe you've felt God's majesty through his forgiveness or through his guidance. Take a few moments to scan your life and look there for God's majesty.

After a few minutes, call kids back together. Ask a few volunteers to share how God's majesty has affected them personally. Then ask:

- **In your life, how have you praised God for the things he's done for you?**

Explain that you're going to have kids respond to God's majesty by creating a praise book. Give each person a piece of paper, and set out markers and pens.

Say: **Write a word or phrase in the middle of your paper that describes how you've experienced God's majesty personally. The word or phrase doesn't have to reveal anything private; it should just mean something to you. Then use your creativity to illustrate what your experience reveals about God's majesty. You can write words, draw pictures, write poems, or do whatever else you can think of. For example, if you experienced God's majesty when he helped you make a decision, you could write a word or phrase about the decision you made, and then you could draw a picture or write a poem that shows how God gives us direction in life. Remember**

God is majestic

that by creating your page, you are praising God for what he's done in your life.

After a few minutes, gather kids together and have them present their work. Ask:

- How does it feel to praise God for what he's done for you?
- What are some other ways you can praise God?
- How can you remember to notice God's majesty all the time?
- How can you remember to respond to God's majesty with praise?

Collect the students' pages, and use a paper punch to put the pages into a three-ring binder. Have kids work together to come up with a title for their praise book. Then say a prayer together, thanking and praising God for each reflection of his majesty that kids described in the book.

Living God's Truth

(5 minutes)

Ask kids to be aware of God's majesty during the upcoming week. Suggest that they keep a piece of paper either at school or beside their beds and every day write about things that make them aware of God's majesty. Also remind kids to take time to praise God every day for those things.

Distribute clean sheets of paper that kids will use to add to the praise book. Ask everyone to create at least one page to add to the book the following week. Encourage kids to explore different ways of expressing praise for God's majesty. For example, they might write a poem or Scripture they read; cut out pictures from magazines; take photographs; quote friends, books, TV shows, or songs; create a natural collage; draw a comic; or collect news articles.

To Follow Up

You might try making a video version of your group's praise book. Bring a video camera to one of your meetings, and allow each person one minute to tape something that reflects God's majesty. You can give the videotape to kids that have video cameras at home so they can take turns adding more segments. If you have a dubbing device on your camera, set your video to music. Or play a contemporary Christian CD while you watch the video with your group.

To Follow Up

Dedicate your book to your church congregation during a worship service. First read aloud Psalm 145, and then have someone discuss God's majesty. Make sure each group member participates by sharing a portion of the book. Then conclude by having the group praise God with the congregation through a song, litany prayer, or additional Scripture reading. Encourage church members to add to the book, and let them know that you'll display the book in a common area of your church.

To Follow Up

For a powerful praise experience, have your kids praise God in a different environment. Take them to a Christian concert or another church's worship service. Be sure to discuss with your kids how the event reflected God's majesty and how others praised God.

About God's Majesty

When ancient Jews said the equivalent of "from A to Z," they meant "from first to last" or "from beginning to end." Therefore, it's significant that Psalm 145 is an acrostic poem, which means each verse begins with a successive letter of the Hebrew alphabet. God himself said in Revelation 1:8: "I am the Alpha and the Omega," the beginning and the end or the first and the last. It's as if the psalmist recognizes this majestic truth about God and uses the acrostic style to praise God's eternal and complete nature.

This psalm of praise reminds us of God's majestic attributes—his greatness, fidelity, compassion—and elicits different responses of praise. "God's kingship is magnificent, his sovereignty beneficent, and his redemptive acts manifold...These perfections are the object of education, proclamation, celebration, and meditation" (Frank E. Gæbelein, ed., et al., *The Expositor's Bible Commentary*). Because God is majestic, we tell others, we tell our children, we sing to God, and we meditate on his mighty acts.

Throughout the poem, the psalmist writes about God's majesty and our only possible response. Because God is great, we praise him. Because God's acts are mighty, we praise him. Because God is slow to anger and rich in love, we praise him. Because God is faithful, we praise him. "In response to this hymnic ascription of praise, the psalmist appropriately concludes...with a vow to praise the Lord...Because the kingdom of God extends to all creation and because the Lord's acts are to all his creation, it is only appropriate that all mankind...must respond to his 'holy name'" (Frank E. Gæbelein, ed., et al., *The Expositor's Bible Commentary*). We are in awe of our perfect God whose majesty is apparent in so many ways. What can we do in return? What else *can* we do? We praise him, we praise him, we praise him!

About God's Majesty

How are we supposed to approach God's majesty? Human beings strive for recognition and approval, but this is not God's way. His majesty has nothing to do with a need for recognition. God is not majestic in order to prove his worth to us. "What is involved here is the divine uniqueness, the right to be acknowledged as supreme...He occupies a solitary throne that allows no place for a rival" (The International Standard Bible Encyclopedia).

Psalm 8, Psalm 9, Psalm 93, Psalm 104, Psalm 145—all of these illustrate God's supremacy. He created everything; he is stronger than everything; he is in control of everything. We can see tangible evidence of his majesty through creation. "He does not leave His creatures without witness. The heavens declare the glory of God both by day and by night...Likewise the elements, thunder and lightning, are pictured as acting in His service...His voice is heard in the thunder, His splendor seen in the lightning. In nature, God presents in tangible form a demonstration of His own power, beauty, and order. These are ingredients of His glory. Things celestial and things terrestrial exhibit the magnificent tapestry that the Creator has woven into His handiwork" (The International Standard Bible Encyclopedia).

While God's majesty can seem enigmatic to us when it's reflected in nature, it can seem obvious when it's reflected in his statutes. Psalm 93:5 says, "Your statutes stand firm; holiness adorns your house for endless days, O Lord." God will always be in control, and he never changes. In a chaotic world, we can see his majesty reflected in his constancy.

So how do we respond? How *can* we respond? When we think about how supreme, how creative, how constant, how loving, how wonderful—how *majestic* God is, we can respond only with praise. "Because God, by his very nature, so far transcends mere human experience, those who encounter his glory, majesty and power are overwhelmed. Furthermore, the limitations of human language—even with poetic figures of speech—do not do justice to such an awesome, holy God" (Quest Study Bible note for Psalm 18:7-15).

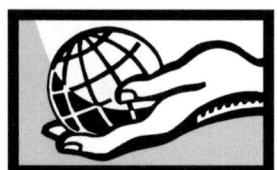

Because God is sovereign,
God has a plan for your life.

Objectives

Through this lesson, students will
- talk about a vacation or trip that went wrong,
- compare making predictions with God's sovereignty,
- make choices and plans for their lives, and
- pray for God's help and direction.

For this lesson, you'll need

- Bibles
- pens
- newsprint
- tape
- a marker
- copies of the "When Things Went Wrong" handout (p. 108)
- copies of the "This Is Your Life" handout (p. 109)
- paper

Understanding God's Sovereignty

According to Forbes magazine's 1998 list of the richest people in America, Bill Gates, the leader of Microsoft Corporation, is the world's richest man, with a net worth of $51 billion. Warren Buffett, the Nebraskan stock market wizard, has $33 billion to his name. Paul Allen has earned $21 billion from his involvement in Microsoft. The money, power, and influence these men command is staggering.

But Solomon, the richest king in Israel's most prosperous period, had power far surpassing Gates, Buffett, and many others combined. Yet when Solomon reflected on all his accomplishments, influence, wealth, and power, he concluded, "Everything is meaningless," and added, "Fear God and keep his commandments, for this is the whole duty of man" (Ecclesiastes 12:8b, 13b). Solomon recognized that the lives of humans are entirely in God's hands.

Your teenagers see an imposing world with an incredible array of choices before them. They may fear the various possibilities ahead. Use this study to help your kids gain the understanding that Solomon had to spend years to find: God is in control of our lives and this earth. And without God's direction and blessing, everything we do is meaningless.

Getting Started

(15 minutes)

Have kids participate in a game show in which they tell about a vacation or trip that went wrong. Form teams of one to three. Give each student a "When Things Went Wrong" handout (p. 108) and a pen. Say: **Has anyone ever seen one of the *Vacation* movies? Think about a time you went on a vacation or trip and things didn't go as planned. Then summarize your experience by filling out the handout.**

Give kids a few minutes to describe their vacation or trip experiences on the handouts. Then say: **It's story time. Each person will share a part or all of his or her vacation story. Please keep offensive material out of the story, but have fun as you tell us what happened.**

Have each student tell his or her experience in one minute. After everyone has finished, say: **You all did a great job of telling your stories!** Ask:
- What were you thinking as you shared your story?
- Why do you think things didn't go as you planned or expected?
- How do you think God feels about situations like these?
- How did you sense God being with you or helping you in your experience?

Say: **Sometimes, our plans go smoothly. Sometimes, poor planning or uncontrollable circumstances interrupt our plans. We're going to explore how God has a plan for our lives. We'll see how God is involved in those plans, even when things seem to be going wrong.**

God Is Sovereign

(20 minutes)

Before your meeting, write the following questions on a sheet of newsprint. Cover the newsprint until you're ready to use it.

1. What things will I accomplish at work?
2. What things will I buy?
3. Who will I meet?
4. What will I do for fun?
5. How will I see God working in my life?

Give each student a sheet of paper. Say: **I want you to write a story about what's going to happen to me next week. On your paper, write the experiences I'll face in the areas indicated on this sheet.**

Display the questions you prepared. Give students about five minutes to write their stories. Then ask:
- **What was it like, trying to predict my experiences?**

Have students share their stories with the group by having each student share his or her prediction for one of the questions listed on the newsprint. After everyone has had a chance to share, ask:
- **How is trying to predict my week like trying to control what will happen in your own life? different?**
- **What things *can* you control in your life? How?**
- **What things *can't* you control? Why not?**

God is sovereign 103

- **How does it feel, knowing you can't control everything that happens in your life?**

Say: **There are many things we can't control in our lives. Fortunately, God has a plan for each of our lives, and he is in complete control. Let's take a minute to explore God's plan and his sovereignty.**

Have teenagers form two groups. Give each group a Bible. Say: **Many years ago, the people of God were conquered by the Babylonians. The prophet Daniel, along with other wise men, served the king, Nebuchadnezzar. One day, the king had a dream that bothered him so much he called all his wise men to interpret the dream. They told the king no person could interpret his strange dream. Nebuchadnezzar was furious and ordered the execution of all the wise men. Before the wise men were killed, Daniel told the king that God could interpret the dream.**

Assign the reading of the dream in Daniel 2:29-35 to one group and the reading of the dream's interpretation in Daniel 2:36-45 to the second group. Have students in each group take turns reading aloud one verse of their assigned passage. Ask:

- **How was the king powerless in this situation?**
- **Why was Daniel's situation different from the king's?**
- **How is God's sovereignty evident in this situation?**

Ask for a volunteer to read Daniel 2:46-49 aloud. Ask:

- **How did God's sovereignty affect Nebuchadnezzar? Daniel?**
- **How can God's sovereignty make a difference in your plans?**

Say: **A powerful king discovered how God's plans revealed God's ultimate power and control over the king's kingdom and future kingdoms. He saw God's sovereignty in a powerful dream. Let's explore how God is sovereign in the plans for your life.**

What That Means for You

(15 minutes)

Have kids prepare a life-planning guide. Give each student a photocopy of the "This Is Your Life" handout (p. 109). Say: **We all face many choices every day, and it may seem hard to know if God is with us when we make those choices. On your handout are several categories of situations and relationships that require choices and plans. At the top of the handout is a Bible passage that shows ways God can guide you. Read the passage, and then write down how you feel God will be with you in the choices and plans you have in each of the areas listed on the handout.**

For Junior High Students

Some of the life-planning areas on the handout may be difficult for junior high students. Help them focus on shorter-range choices to make this activity more meaningful to them.

Give kids ten minutes to complete their handouts. Then ask:
- **Was it easy or difficult to think about your plans or choices? Explain.**
- **In what ways did you discover that God is with you in your choices or plans?**
- **How will knowing this help you face plans that go wrong?**

Say: **God's sovereignty extends to each of our lives. As we make plans, we can know that God is the most important part of those plans. Now, let's each ask God to guide us in one of our plans.**

Living God's Truth
(5 minutes)

Say: **At the beginning of the meeting, we told stories about trips that went wrong. Look over your "This Is Your Life" handout. Think about a time something went wrong in an important area of your life. Recall how you saw God working in that situation. On the back of your handout, write a prayer thanking God for his presence with you.**

Give kids about three minutes to complete their prayers. Say: **Just as King Nebuchadnezzar found out about God's sovereignty in his life, your experiences of God's presence through difficult times can assure you of God's continued plans for your life. Think about where you were and what your life was like one year ago. On the back of your handout, write a few sentences that explain how God has taken care of you over the past year. Then try to identify his plan and purpose for you for the past year.**

After a minute, ask:
- **How has God worked in your life over the past year?**
- **Do you believe that God will work in your life next year? If so, how?**
- **Do you have an idea of what God's plan for your life may be? Explain.**

Say: **Even when things don't go the way you want, God has a plan for your life. No matter what happens, God is with you and is ready to guide you. Let's take a moment to thank him for his sovereignty.**

To close, have kids pray short prayers similar to his one: "Dear God, thank you for being in control of my life. Please show me your plan for my life. Please help me understand what I should do in the following area of my life…"

To Follow Up

Have kids interview their parents or other mature Christians about the plans God has revealed to them. Encourage kids to ask about situations in which the person's plans didn't go as expected.

To Follow Up

Have students write a letter to God about all their worries. Have kids address the letters to themselves. Hold on to the letters for about a week; then mail the letters to the kids. During your next meeting, ask students how God has worked out his plans concerning their worries.

Bible Insight

When Nebuchadnezzar asked Daniel if he could interpret his dream, Daniel exalted God by asserting, "there is a God in heaven who reveals mysteries," affirming the truth of God's power over the pagan gods and seers. The unusual dream consisted of a huge statue made of four metals: a gold head, a silver chest and arms, a bronze belly, and iron legs. Additionally the statue had feet made of iron and clay. The statue was crushed by a huge rock that took the place of the statue and grew into a huge mountain, filling the earth (verses 26-35).

Daniel immediately gave a detailed interpretation of the dream (verses 36-45). The five sections of the statue represented four world kingdoms. Daniel began with Nebuchadnezzar's own kingdom, Babylon. This was the head of gold, which was a fitting description of Nebuchadnezzar's kingdom—he exercised supreme control over all the laws and everyone's existence. Yet Daniel reminded the king that it was God who gave him the right to be "king of kings" (verse 36), a fact Nebuchadnezzar forgot to his own peril (see Daniel 4:28-37).

The silver chest represented the second kingdom following Babylon and was called inferior. Cyrus the Great conquered Babylon in 539 B.C., ushering in the kingdom of the Medo-Persians. The empire reached its peak under Darius but failed to handle the Greeks on Persia's western border. The kingdom ruled the Near and Middle East for about two centuries.

The Greeks conquered the Medes and Persians, bringing in the reign of the third kingdom, represented by bronze on the statue. Each successive kingdom was viewed dimly by Nebuchadnezzar, thus the progressive decline in metal quality of his dream's statue. The Greeks were indeed to "rule over all the earth," as Alexander the Great conquered Persia in 331 B.C., and his kingdom extended from Yugoslavia to India. Alexander died shortly after his victory, and his empire eventually split into four kingdoms.

The fourth kingdom was Rome, and Roman power to crush opponents befitted the image of iron in the dream. The Roman empire gradually took over the separate kingdoms of the Greeks, with the victory over Egypt in 31 B.C. bringing an end to the nearly three hundred years of Greek world rule. The image of the fourth kingdom was in two sections; the legs of iron represented the Roman Empire in its glory under Emperor Trajan (A.D. 98-117). The feet of iron mixed with clay probably represented the weaknesses of the Roman socialist society and the unstable nature of an empire in moral decay.

The final image in the dream was a "rock cut out of a mountain, but not by human hands," representing the eternal kingdom established by God. In opposition to the four earthly kingdoms that ruled for a few centuries, God's kingdom crushed and overwhelmed them all.

About God's Sovereignty

The term "sovereignty" describes a situation in which a person's innate dignity exercises supreme power. As applied to God, the term indicates his complete power over creation, so that his will is carried out without regard for the finite will of others. Although the term does not occur in the Bible, it is implied mostly with the usage of a ruler and subject metaphor, such as that used in Daniel 4:25.

Humans were granted sovereignty over nature (Genesis 2:15). Later, kings were given rule by God's mandate. The sovereignty God gives humans is conditional—it may be revoked (1 Samuel 15:11). The choices made by humans, whether good or bad, may lead God to exercise restraint in the sovereignty he grants. God's sovereignty is not limited, though he may sometimes exercise restraint in its use.

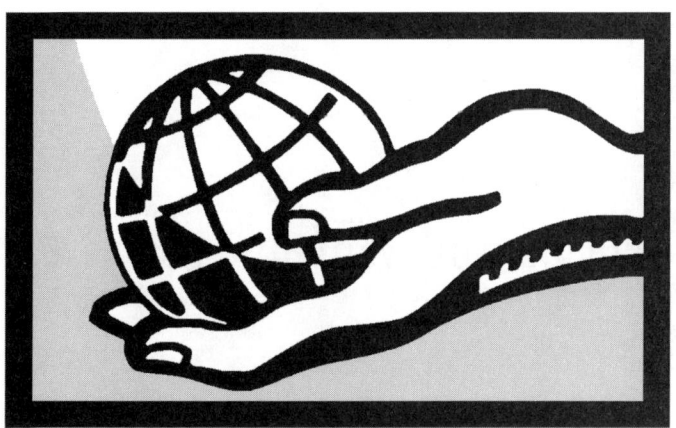

When Things Went Wrong

Instructions: Think about the last vacation or trip you took that went wrong. Prepare a brief story about the experience by answering the following questions:

1. Who joined you on the trip?

2. Where were you going?

3. How long were you gone?

4. Was this trip one you wanted to go on? Explain.

5. Did things go exactly as planned? Explain.

6. Who or what helped you when things went wrong?

7. How did the trip end?

This Is Your Life

Instructions: **Read Psalm 23.** List all the choices you're facing or plans you have in each of the areas listed below. Write one way you see God leading you through each plan or choice.

1. School
Plans or choices:

How God is leading me:

2. Family
Plans or choices:

How God is leading me:

3. Friends
Plans or choices:

How God is leading me:

4. Jobs or career
Plans or choices:

How God is leading me:

5. Other situations
Plans or choices:

How God is leading me:

Exciting Resources for Your Youth Ministry

All-Star Games From All-Star Youth Leaders

The ultimate game book—from the biggest names in youth ministry! All-time no-fail favorites from Wayne Rice, Les Christie, Rich Mullins, Tiger McLuen, Darrell Pearson, Dave Stone, Bart Campolo, Steve Fitzhugh, and 21 others! You get all the games you'll need for any situation. Plus, you get practical advice about how to design your own games and tricks for turning a *good* game into a *great* game!

ISBN 0-7644-2020-8

Last Impressions: Unforgettable Closings for Youth Meetings

Make the closing moments of your youth programs powerful and memorable with this collection of Group's best-ever low-prep (or no-prep!) youth meeting closings. You get over 170 favorite closings, each tied to a thought-provoking Bible passage. Great for anyone who works with teenagers!

ISBN 1-55945-629-9

The Youth Worker's Encyclopedia of Bible-Teaching Ideas

Here are the most comprehensive idea-books available for youth workers. With more than 365 creative ideas in each of these 400-page encyclopedias, there's at least one idea for every book of the Bible. You'll find ideas for retreats and overnighters...learning games...adventures...special projects...affirmations...parties...prayers...music...devotions...skits...and more!

Old Testament   ISBN 1-55945-184-X
New Testament   ISBN 1-55945-183-1

PointMaker™ Devotions for Youth Ministry

These 45 PointMakers™ help your teenagers discover, understand, and apply biblical principles. Use PointMakers as brief meetings on specific topics or slide them into any youth curriculum to make a lasting impression. Includes handy Scripture and topical indexes that make it quick and easy to select the perfect PointMaker for any lesson you want to teach!

ISBN 0-7644-2003-8

Order today from your local Christian bookstore, or write: Group Publishing, P.O. Box 485, Loveland, CO 80539.

More Resources for Your Youth Ministry

Group's Best Discussion Launchers for Youth Ministry

Here's the definitive collection of Group's best-ever discussion launchers! You'll get hundreds of thought-provoking questions kids can't resist discussing...compelling quotes that demand a response...and quick activities that pull kids into an experience they can't wait to talk about. Add zing to your youth meetings...revive meetings that are drifting off-track...and comfortably approach sensitive topics like AIDS, war, cults, gangs, suicide, dating, parents, self-image, and more!

ISBN 0-7644-2023-2

You-Choose-the-Ending Skits for Youth Ministry

Stephen Parolini

Try these 19 hot-topic skits guaranteed to keep your kids on the edge of their seats—because each skit has 3 possible endings! You can choose the ending...flip a coin...or let your teenagers vote. No matter which ending you pick, you'll get a great discussion going about a topic kids care about! Included: no-fail discussion questions!

ISBN 1-55945-627-2

No Supplies Required Crowdbreakers & Games

Dan McGill

This is the perfect book for youth workers on a tight budget. The only supplies you'll need for these quick activities are kids! All 95 ideas are fun, easy-to-do, creative, and tested for guaranteed success!

ISBN 1-55945-700-7

Youth Worker's Idea Depot™

Practical, proven ideas gathered from front-line professionals make this CD-ROM a gold mine of ministry solutions! You can search these ideas instantly—by Scripture...topic...key words...or by personal notes you've entered into your database. You'll get a complete library of ideas—plus a trial subscription to Group Magazine, where you'll discover dozens of new ideas in every issue! For Windows 3.1 or Windows 95.

ISBN 0-7644-2034-8

Order today from your local Christian bookstore, or write: Group Publishing, P.O. Box 485, Loveland, CO 80539.